Reinventing Diplomacy
in the Information Age

Reinventing Diplomacy in the Information Age

A Report of the CSIS Advisory Panel on Diplomacy in the Information Age

Project cochairs

Richard Burt
Olin Robison

Project director

Barry Fulton

December 1998

About CSIS

The Center for Strategic and International Studies (CSIS), established in 1962, is a private, tax-exempt institution focusing on international public policy issues. Its research is nonpartisan and nonproprietary.

CSIS is dedicated to policy impact. It seeks to inform and shape selected policy decisions in government and the private sector to meet the increasingly complex and difficult global challenges that leaders will confront in the next century. It achieves this mission in three ways: by generating strategic analysis that is anticipatory and interdisciplinary; by convening policymakers and other influential parties to assess key issues; and by building structures for policy action.

CSIS does not take specific public policy positions. Accordingly, all views, positions, and conclusions expressed in this publication should be understood to be solely those of the authors.

Library of Congress Cataloging-in-Publication Data

Reinventing diplomacy in the information age / Richard Burt and Olin Robison, project
  cochairs ; Barry Fulton, project director.
    p.   cm. — (CSIS panel reports, ISSN 0899-0352)
    ISBN 0-89206-346-7
    1. United States—Foreign relations—1993—Data processing.   2. United States.   Dept. of
State—Automation.   3. Diplomacy—Technological innovations.   I. Burt, Richard.   II. Robison,
Olin.   III. Fulton, Barry.   IV. Series.
JZ1480.R45   1998
327.73'00285—dc21
                                                                              98-54239
                                                                                 CIP

The CSIS Press
Center for Strategic and International Studies
1800 K Street, NW, Washington, DC 20006
Telephone: (202) 887-0200; Fax: (202) 775-3199
E-mail: books@csis.org
Web site: http://www.csis.org/

Contents

Foreword

FOR THREE DECADES the Center for Strategic and International Studies (CSIS) has directed its attention and analysis to the conduct of U.S. diplomacy. We have focused much of our effort on public diplomacy and international broadcasting. The Panel on International Information, Education, and Cultural Relations, better known as the Stanton Panel, was hosted by CSIS. Its recommendations led to the consolidation of the State Department's Bureau of Educational and Cultural Affairs with the United States Information Agency and still have resonance today.

This new study, *Reinventing Diplomacy in the Information Age*, was initiated by CSIS to advance the conduct of U.S. diplomacy in the next century. It is a study neither of foreign policy nor of institutional structure. Instead, it examines the new international dynamics, identifies performance gaps, and proposes a strategy for change. The study argues that diplomacy must become increasingly public to serve the national interest.

A 63-person advisory panel, focusing on the Information Revolution, the widening participation of publics in international relations, and the concurrent revolutions in global business and finance, has put forth a bold agenda. Because so many practices of twentieth-century diplomacy are threatened with irrelevance, the panel has called for reinvention. With a new culture, new technologies, new media, and new relationships, the foreign affairs community will be ready for a counterpart to the Pentagon's revolution in military affairs. The recommendations herein constitute the minimal requirements for a revolution in diplomatic affairs. The architecture for the revolution will require, as well, a reexamination of policymaking and of organizational relationships.

In my 35 years with CSIS, I cannot recall a panel that has worked with such harmony and resolve. Its distinguished members came here from government service, higher education, journalism, and the business and NGO communities to offer advice on how to strengthen America's diplomacy. Over a period of 15 months they reached the consensus you will find in this study. With the discerning leadership of cochairs Richard Burt and Olin Robison, as well as Hodding Carter who served in that role for the first several months, the panel has produced an extremely useful report.

I am proud to endorse it and commend it to the administration and Congress for their consideration and action. The study concludes with the admonition that U.S. diplomacy "must be guided by coherence, capability, discipline, and agility. It must be characterized by openness and permeability. It must change now." I trust you will agree.

David M. Abshire
President, CSIS

Preface

AMERICAN DIPLOMACY IS TODAY AT SEVERE RISK because it does not have the modern technology it needs to do its job. As astonishing as it may seem, the Department of State does not have the proper tools for gathering, processing, and disseminating information, nor for communicating effectively with an increasingly democratic world.

All this has happened at precisely the historical moment when U.S. technological innovation leads and shapes the globalization process, both at home and abroad. All this has happened during a decade when the international affairs budget has been cut by more than 20 percent. Embassies have been closed, U.S. diplomats have been recalled, and the communications infrastructure has been neglected.

From Ireland to Israel, from South Africa to Indonesia—the United States must continue to provide some measure of stability in a world that remains unpredictable and turbulent. Yet, there is an anomaly in our conduct of diplomacy. Its instruments are left over from another era. Although the image of a diplomat in striped pants is nothing but a stereotype from the past, the hierarchical cable culture that defines U.S. diplomacy today has changed little in the last century. Not only must American diplomacy be brought up to date, it must reflect the nation's position of global leadership. The stakes are too high to do otherwise.

We are honored to have chaired an advisory panel of 63 concerned citizens—former diplomats, journalists, academicians, representatives from the nongovernmental organizations and business, and others who have been long involved in public life. Over a period of 15 months they have freely given their time to consider, discuss, and propose solutions to the challenges that face U.S. diplomacy in the next century. Without exception, the members of the panel agree that bold steps must be taken to reverse the deterioration of U.S. diplomacy.

None will be satisfied if this report simply takes its place alongside other thoughtful reports that have called for change. This is a call for swift and essential action. We hope the administration and Congress will move quickly to consider and even expand the strategies for change.

The United States cannot depend solely on its economic and military preeminence to ensure that it fulfills its responsibilities for global leadership. We cannot afford second-class diplomacy, which will be inevitable without first-class technology and its imaginative use.

Richard Burt
Project Cochair

Olin Robison
Project Cochair

Acknowledgments

WITH TALK OF CONSOLIDATION IN THE AIR, Leonard Marks and Barry Zorthian proposed to CSIS president David Abshire in 1996 that it was time to reconsider the future of public diplomacy. He greeted the proposal with enthusiasm and expanded it to a study for transforming the conduct of U.S. diplomacy. A 63-person advisory panel was invited to oversee the study that would focus on the Information Revolution, the widening participation of publics in international relations, and the concurrent revolutions in global business and finance.

The advisory panel was convened by cochairs Richard Burt and Hodding Carter in mid-1997 and met five times to consider and discuss the requirements for U.S. diplomacy in the next century. Midway through the study, when Hodding Carter assumed new duties as a foundation president, he was succeeded as cochair by Olin Robison. Without exception, all members of the panel have remained engaged for more than a year, giving freely of their time and ideas. Attendance at meetings has swelled as the study came to a conclusion. The members of the panel deeply care about restoring diplomacy's lost luster.

Of the many institutions and individuals to be acknowledged, the Annenberg Foundation merits special thanks for funding the study, and USIA for seconding the project director to CSIS. Cochairs Richard Burt and Olin Robison have given generously of their time to shape the study. Walter Roberts, who served as project director of the Stanton Panel two decades ago, is recognized for his shrewd insights. Barry Zorthian has unfailingly offered wise advice.

Diana Lady Dougan and Bill Garrison are thanked for their personal interest and the generous support of the International Communications Studies Program. Erik Peterson, too, warrants appreciation for his contributions on global economics. Tony Quainton, recently retired from the Department of State, brought enormous breadth and common sense to the study. Chuck Schmitz, skeptical of easy rhetoric and pat solutions, relentlessly pushed to sharpen the study. Larry Grossman provided thoughtful and provocative insights. Kevin Klose contributed his editorial talents to the executive summary. Sandy Ungar, in his masterful editing of the report, gave more time than we had any right to expect.

Milda Hedblom and Kenneth Keller did all of the preparation for the conference in Minneapolis. Likewise, Jonathan Aronson and Geoff Cowan planned the Los Angeles conference. Neither of these events would have been possible without them. Peter Schwartz enlivened the debate with his presentation on future international scenarios. Morley Winograd, who is directing the reinvention of the federal government, inspired the advisory panel to direct its attention to the vision and values of diplomacy.

Appreciation is extended to Chris Foss for providing computer support and editing transcriptions. Valuable assistance in transcription and administrative support was also given by Jacqueline Hansmann, Ann Stark, and Kevin Hartmann. Student interns Noriko Akashi, Elisabetta Malcontenti, and Jill Rothenbueler also generously assisted with the project.

The contributions of several other institutions are acknowledged as well, not least of which is the report, *A New Diplomacy for the Information Age,* issued by the U.S. Advisory Commission on Public Diplomacy under the chairmanship of Lewis Manilow. It called for a new diplomacy based on the Information Revolution and the growing power of foreign publics. *Financing America's Leadership*, sponsored by the Brookings Institution and the Council on Foreign Relations, called for an increase in resources, strong leadership, and the reform of U.S. foreign affairs agencies. *Who Needs Embassies?*, published by Georgetown University's Institute for the Study of Diplomacy, examined the role of U.S. embassies in five key countries and documented the consequences of shrinking resources in an increasingly complex world. It called for a national consensus on the U.S. role in the world and on the resources that are devoted to shaping it. A major conference on virtual diplomacy, organized by the United States Institute of Peace, explored the new challenges of international conflict management in the Information Age. An international conference, "Diplomacy: Profession in Crisis?", held at Wilton Park, also examined the new requirements for conducting relations between states.

Concurrent with the CSIS study, the Henry L. Stimson Center initiated its project on the advocacy of U.S. interests abroad, which has resulted in *Equipped for the Future: Managing U.S. Foreign Affairs in the 21st Century.* As the two studies progressed, we shared ideas and research. Consequently, both studies have benefited. Although we have taken different approaches, we have reached conclusions that are complementary.

Finally, a personal word of thanks to the many advisory panel members who inspired a consensus on the strategies leading to the reinvention of diplomacy. At the panel's first meeting, Rita Hauser asked if the panel was prepared to address how diplomacy must change: "Are we going to tinker around the edges or come to the heart of the matter?" The advisory panel wisely decided not to tinker around the edges.

Barry Fulton
Project Director
October 1998

Executive Summary

THE CSIS ADVISORY PANEL CALLS FOR REINVENTING the conduct of diplomacy in the Information Age. With a focus on the Information Revolution, the widening participation of publics in international relations, and the concurrent revolutions in global business and finance, the panel recommends sweeping changes in the Department of State and other foreign affairs agencies.

International Dynamics

The world is changing fundamentally. Images and information respect neither time nor borders. Hierarchy is giving way to networking. Openness is crowding out secrecy and exclusivity. Ideas and capital move swiftly and unimpeded across a global network of governments, corporations, and nongovernmental organizations. In this world of instantaneous information, traditional diplomacy struggles to sustain its relevance.

Fundamental forces that demand change in the practice of U.S. diplomacy include:

- Revolution in information technology,

- Proliferation of new media,

- Globalization of business and finance,

- Widening participation of publics in international relations, and

- Complex issues that transcend national boundaries.

The prime mover of change is information technology. When Gutenberg shattered the old order by mechanizing printing five centuries ago, the democratization of literacy and knowledge irresistibly followed. As the millennium ends, the microchip is again revolutionizing information gathering and transmission and will bring even more profound changes in the next century. The critical elements are the international networks created by computers and electronic connectivity. Exponential growth in computing power and plummeting international telecommunications costs are having profound consequences for finance, business, education, medicine, civil society, and government. Nations once connected by foreign ministries and traders are now linked through millions of individuals by fiber optics, satellite, wireless, and cable in a complex network without central control. The Internet, with 100 million users today, will reach one billion people by 2005 and will be available to half the world's population by 2010. The network will become the central nervous system of international relations.

The new media, born of the Information Age with low entry costs and global distribution, are available to anyone with creativity and a modest investment. Electronic entrepreneurs are challenging the dominance of the old media controlled by states and corporations. A new Web site is created every 4 seconds. Newspapers from practically every country in the world are freely available at our desktops. Radio programs and full-motion video are accessible through the Internet. The Internet itself—connected through telephone, cable, wireless, or satellite links—can be accessed on personal computers, personal digital assistants, and even home television sets. The media are converging, combining print, audio, and video to offer a staggering choice of information and entertainment. The gatekeepers are being eliminated as the transition from mass to customized media accelerates.

Globalization of finance and business has erased national boundaries from the laws of supply and demand. More than a trillion dollars a day are exchanged in international money markets with little or no state intervention. International commerce is fueling the U.S. economy. By 2002, electronic commerce, now in its infancy, will exceed $300 billion a year. The constraints of distance are disappearing in the information economy. Markets are becoming more efficient but also more volatile. Spurred by government research that led to Intelsat and the Internet, U.S. innovation has created a new information economy that could continue its surge for decades. Although some argue that most nations will benefit from globalization, fears range from a growing gap between rich and poor to the loss of U.S. jobs to the developing countries. As the world struggles to come to terms with the economic crises in East Asia and Russia, few doubt that the changes under way are consequential.

The public dimension receives less attention, yet it may be the most significant of the changes that affect the conduct of diplomacy. Virtually no major foreign affairs or domestic initiative is taken today without first testing public opinion. The public dimension includes not only public opinion, which has long been recognized as essential, but also public consultation, involvement, and action. From China to Chiapas, ordinary members of the public are developing new competencies for global engagement. More than 15,000 NGOs are directly involved in international issues. Private initiatives, such as Ted Turner's creation of the $1 billion United Nations Foundation and George Soros's pledge of $500 million to Russia, are having profound effects on public policy. The public dimension is becoming the central element of the new diplomacy and a critical influence on foreign policy.

The Information Age poses intense new challenges to our diplomacy, either magnifying international disagreement and discord or distracting people from vital concerns abroad. The consequences can be fast and deadly. The dominant issues of the next decade include democracy and human rights; weapons of mass destruction; terrorism, drugs, and global crime; environmental concerns; population, refugees, and migration; disease and famine. The Information Age increases the relevance of these issues to the peoples of the world. The penalty to America's diplomacy for inattention will be severe.

The Performance Gap

Diplomacy is the art of advancing national interests through the sustained exchange of information among nations and peoples. Its purpose is to change attitudes and behavior. It is the practice of state-to-state persuasion.

Classic diplomacy assumes that sovereign states control international relations. However, faced with technologies that empower contradictory impulses of fragmentation and integration and generate instant and often uncontrolled, unmediated problems, diplomacy in the twenty-first century must overturn its culture of secrecy and its penchant for exclusivity.

The conduct of U.S. diplomacy faces unacceptable performance gaps between its outdated practices and the requirements of the new age of information. These gaps include diplomatic priorities, professional standards, leadership, infrastructure, resources, telecommunications, computers, media deployment, and relations with the media, business, and NGO communities. In short, the State Department and allied agencies are encumbered with traditions and tools that inhibit the practice of diplomacy.

The gaps in diplomatic performance have consequences. Whether it be the contagion of economic collapse that started in Bangkok or the massacre of civilians in Kosovo, U.S. diplomacy must be given the means to alert the international community and modulate the turbulence that threatens international order.

Other elements of the federal government, including the Department of Defense, have embraced reform. It is time for the foreign affairs community to take this path as well, faced as it is with declining resources and the need to refocus after a half century of the Cold War at the center of U.S. concerns. Effective leadership by the United States in sustaining international stability depends upon the ability of our foreign affairs agencies to change and adapt to the imperatives of the Information Age. U.S. diplomacy must be empowered with the tools and techniques of the twenty-first century. Without change, our diplomacy is threatened with irrelevance.

To act effectively, the United States will require coalitions with other nations, NGOs, and corporations. There are few recent examples of success in foreign policy where the United States acted alone—and none where the United States government acted successfully without the support of the American public. Because the U.S. economy requires global security and prosperity, every citizen has a stake in the conduct of U.S. diplomacy. Genocide in Rwanda, war in Kosovo, financial chaos in Indonesia, nuclear tests in India and Pakistan, the population explosion in Mexico—all are threats to international stability and to the livelihood of U.S. workers.

A Strategy for Change

The culture of diplomacy must be overhauled to make it more accessible and participatory; obsolete technology must be discarded and replaced to make diplomacy more efficient and relevant; and a larger community of international and domestic actors must be included in deliberations and implementation. These changes will require bold and sustained leadership as well as a better-trained, more effective diplomatic service.

A plan of action[1] to reinvent U.S. diplomatic practice must be developed under the direction of the secretary of state. Efficiencies, adjustments, and half measures will not suffice.

---

1. For details, see "For All of This to Happen..." beginning on page 75.

- Appoint a senior executive team—under the direction of the secretary of State—from State, USAID, USIA, Commerce, Agriculture, and other agencies that deal in foreign affairs to undertake the management of change.

- Form a management advisory council of distinguished representatives from the business, academic, government, and NGO communities to advise the foreign affairs community on implementing change strategies.

- Establish a compact with Congress to promote change, including the amendment of Smith-Mundt.

- Announce new and more rigorous standards for the appointment of political and career ambassadors to signal a renewal of professionalism and a redelegation of authority to embassies.

- Establish an ambitious and detailed timeline for change; make use of benchmarking and best-practices techniques.

- Reverse the decade-long decline in resources for the conduct of diplomacy.

Summary of Recommendations

The advisory panel recommends six substantive strategies to prepare U.S. diplomacy for the next century. Summarized below, they include key recommendations from the text of the report.

Create a More Accessible Environment[2]

Ending the culture of secrecy and exclusivity is a requirement for developing a collaborative relationship with the public.

- Encourage public awareness and participation through bold leadership.

- Reform the culture of diplomacy by discouraging secrecy and exclusivity.

- Reorder diplomatic priorities by stressing program management and advocacy.

- Develop a broader array of professional relationships through networking.

- Give more attention to international and domestic public opinion.

- Balance the requirements of security and openness.

Adopt a Disciplined Coordination Model for the Conduct of Diplomacy[3]

The hierarchical control model of the past should be replaced by distributed decision-making, delegated authority, and bureaucratic streamlining.

- Adopt a new paradigm that recognizes the distinctive roles of various agencies.

---

2. See page 53 for details.
3. See page 57 for details.

- Develop a disciplined business plan that rewards excellence.
- Designate stakeholders.
- Identify constituents.
- Strengthen frontline diplomacy.
- Reach agreement on a statement of vision and values.

Lead a Renaissance of Professionalism[4]

Replacing outdated practices of workforce management, creating new professional opportunities, and making a commitment to sustained professional development are required to change the existing culture.

- Reform the career service.
- Create a reserve service.
- Establish virtual regional and functional teams.
- Overhaul workforce planning and management.
- Encourage joint service through exchanges with other agencies.
- Require continuing professional development.

Upgrade Information Technology to Corporate Standards[5]

The acquisition of new technologies must be geared to supporting the key priorities of diplomacy.

- Develop an information strategy to advance national interests.
- Modernize telecommunications.
- Upgrade and customize computers.
- Develop a foreign affairs network.
- Designate and attend to key users of information technologies.
- Provide information technology resources commensurate with needs.

Move Public Diplomacy from the Sidelines to the Core of Diplomacy[6]

Diplomacy must be proactive in promoting U.S. policies and values and interactive in engaging domestic and foreign publics.

- Redefine public diplomacy.
- Repeal those portions of Smith-Mundt that prohibit domestic dissemination.
- Strengthen relations with the NGO community.

---

4. See page 60 for details.
5. See page 64 for details.
6. See page 68 for details.

- Strengthen relations with the academic community.

- Improve media relations domestically and internationally.

- Modernize broadcasting with a global affairs channel and new surge capacity.

Focus Greater Attention and Place a Higher Priority on Commercial Diplomacy[7]

To ensure U.S. competitiveness in the global economy, the United States must strengthen its ability to expand global markets and assist U.S. business abroad.

- Improve the status of commercial officers, including private sector exchanges.

- Strengthen the ambassador's role as advocate for improving commercial ties.

- Establish U.S. business and information centers in the big emerging markets.

- Establish a global center for commerce and finance.

- Provide more resources to the Office of the U.S. Trade Representative to strengthen global negotiations.

- Maintain support for multilateral diplomacy through international organizations.

Despite the many promises of the Information Age, the world in which diplomacy operates remains a dangerous place. Failure to respond to the imperatives of change threatens U.S. security and prosperity as well as U.S. respect for humanity. U.S. diplomacy must be guided by coherence, capability, discipline, and agility. It must be characterized by openness and permeability. It must change now.

---

7. See page 71 for details.

Introduction

THE AMERICAN CENTURY HAS BEEN DEFINED IN LARGE PART by its technologies as the industrial age matured and the information age blossomed. The early hope that electricity, motion pictures, and radio would improve communication across cultural and national boundaries is echoed today by the Internet and the new digital technologies. Unlike the mass media that they are challenging, these new technologies are diffuse, profoundly democratic, and highly resistant to central control. Everyone can become a publisher and a broadcaster. Individual expression is flourishing with little restraint. Linear, hierarchical, command-and-control systems are being subverted by complex social and economic networks. It is a time for celebration as cherished American values—freedom, individualism, opportunity—are reinforced by the new technologies. It is an opportunity for reassessing America's international engagement.

Never before have so many nations embraced democracy. Never before have borders been so open to the flow of ideas and images. The opportunities for advancing the goals of American foreign policy are unprecedented. Yet the United States paradoxically is circumscribed by its failure to forge a new bipartisan foreign policy and by the growing gaps in its conduct of diplomacy—its diplomatic culture, technology, and relations with key constituents. The diplomatic-cable culture will inevitably give way to the evolving digital culture; but if changes in information processing are not accelerated, U.S. diplomacy risks being rendered irrelevant. In its arms control negotiations with the Soviet Union during the past decade, the United States wisely placed the highest priority on transparency; however, within the foreign affairs community itself, secrecy and exclusivity still take precedence.

> The qualities of the digital revolution, its dynamism, its curiosity, its flexibility and its drive—they're at the core of our character and the legacy of our original revolution.
> —Bill Clinton

The stability of large systems—nations, alliances, international coalitions—depends in large part on efficient and accurate channels of communication among the constituent parts of the system. When the Department of State controlled many of the channels of international communication between nations, it could well afford to be parsimonious in sharing information outside of Foggy Bottom. Today, as the channels available to the federal government constitute an increasingly smaller share of the total, it is imperative that government communications be both trusted and efficient. Otherwise the role of government in modulating international turbulence will shrink. The United States must not only reflect its national values by insisting on conceptual

> Over the next two generations we will have a scale of rethinking and reorganizing how we engage in international relations, which will be comparable to the early sixteenth century in terms of the rise of what we now call diplomacy.
> —Newt Gingrich

1

coherence in its foreign policy but must also ensure that the conduct of diplomacy is consonant with its purpose. Diplomacy must expand its reach from a closed circle of knowledgeable diplomats to a much broader circle of interested Americans and, as well, to those publics abroad who influence global decisionmaking.

The Westphalian world in which modern diplomacy was born is no longer recognizable. Although Marshall McLuhan's global village has not replaced the nation-state, the villages are so thoroughly interconnected that capital and ideas increasingly move unimpeded across borders. If "sudden extensions of communication are reflected in cultural disturbances,"[1] as Canadian scholar Harold Innis observed a half century ago, there appears to be wide agreement that we are experiencing a cultural disturbance of global proportions.

> The new information technologies are already influencing the conduct of diplomacy. Embassies are being bypassed in this globalized environment of instant interactivity, disintermediation, individual empowerment, and networked information.
>
> —Diana Lady Dougan

Networking is overtaking hierarchy and bureaucracy as a primary mode of organization and communication. Governments that fail to yield control place their nations at risk. For example, Nigeria fell into economic ruin under military control; and North Korea, insistent on maintaining its political hierarchy and command economy, has faced mass starvation.

The Communist revolution is over. The microchip revolution is changing international relations—as we observe the contradictory trends of global integration and fragmentation. International affairs scholar James Rosenau describes the central characteristic of world politics today as "persistent tensions between tendencies toward integration and those that foster fragmentation."[2] Political scientist Benjamin Barber asserts that "the planet is falling precipitously apart and coming reluctantly together at the very same moment."[3] Diplomatic historian John Lewis

> I'm increasingly convinced that the future progress of democracy and human rights will depend at least as much on the Internet and on the communications revolution as it will on official American government policies in pushing other societies towards reform.
>
> —Anthony Lake

Gaddis, too, suggests that the international competition that is emerging "could be just as stark and just as pervasive as was the rivalry between democracy and totalitarianism at the height of the Cold War: it is the contest between the forces of integration and fragmentation in the contemporary international environment."[4] U.S. diplomacy faces a transformative moment the equal of any in its history.

The several elements that impel changes in the practice of diplomacy include the revolution in information technology, the proliferation of new media, globalization of business and finance, and increasing participation of publics in international relations. The issues with which diplomacy must deal are increasingly diverse, complex, and interdependent. The United States can neither understand nor respond to any one without reference to the others.

1. Harold A. Innis, *The Bias of Communication* (Toronto: University of Toronto Press, 1951), 31.
2. James N. Rosenau, "Security in a Turbulent World," *Current History* (May 1995): 194.
3. Benjamin R. Barber, *Jihad vs. McWorld* (New York: Times Books, 1995), 4.
4. John Lewis Gaddis, "Toward the Post–Cold War World," *Foreign Affairs* (Spring 1991): 103.

CHAPTER I

International Dynamics

Information Technology

"DOES MICROSOFT HAVE A FOREIGN POLICY?" Columnist Tom Friedman posed the question in the *New York Times* a few years ago and concluded that "U.S. foreign policy will be shaped to a significant degree by decisions taken in Washington—Redmond, Washington."[5] Writing in *Foreign Affairs* on "America's Information Edge," Harvard professor Joseph Nye and Admiral William Owens demonstrate that the U.S. information edge can be a "force multiplier of American diplomacy."[6]

Few would dispute that technology is changing diplomacy. Absent a consensus on the meaning of this change, however, the challenge is to go beyond the clichés of connectivity and describe the means by which technology may change diplomacy. Is everything just faster but otherwise the same? Or does faster by factors of 100, 1000, or more constitute substantive change?

There are two complementary technologies that account for the changes we are witnessing: computers and telecommunications. In 1965 Gordon Moore, the cofounder of Intel, forecast that computing power would double every 18 months. Moore's law has held for more than 30 years and will continue to bring the price of computing downward for at least another decade. Today's personal computers (PCs), selling for less than $1,000, operate 10 times faster than a 1970 IBM mainframe computer that sold for nearly $5 million.[7] By 2010, prices will have plunged to less than $100.

The cost of telecommunications has not yet dropped as dramatically although the decline is accelerating owing to fiber-optic cables, satellites, digitization, and deregulation. When first introduced in 1915, a 3-minute phone call from New York to San Francisco cost more than $20, or the equivalent of 90 hours of labor for the average wage earner.[8] Today 2 minutes of work will pay for the call. When the cell phone was

> This is not like the information revolution, say, of the 30s, which was a revolution in which Hitler and Mussolini and other people could shout at you in big crowds. This is an information revolution where they can talk back.
>
> —Lewis Manilow

> One of the major points I want to get across is the profundity of the changes the Net will bring to human institutions—and its lack of impact on human nature.
>
> —Esther Dyson

---

5. Thomas L. Friedman, "Foreign Policy 3.1," *New York Times*, October 8, 1995.

6. Joseph S. Nye, Jr. and William A. Owens, "America's Information Edge," *Foreign Affairs* (March/April 1996): 20.

7. W. Michael Cox and Richard Alm, *Time Well Spent: The Declining Real Cost of Living in America*, 1997 Annual Report of the Dallas Federal Reserve Bank (Dallas: Federal Reserve Bank, 1998), 18 <http://www.dallasfed.org/publications.ar/pdf/ar_current.pdf>.

introduced in 1984, Motorola sold a single instrument for more than $4,000.[9] Today cell phones are given away as an inducement for signing a service contract. And within a decade, after deregulation, the cost of an international telephone call will be well below the 10-cents-per-minute charge now available to consumers within the United States. The actual cost to providers is already less than 1 cent.

> The greatest impact will be the new wireless infrastructure. The digital information age will change the way content is created and produced.
> —Charles Z. Wick

When these two technologies—computers and telecommunications—are integrated to constitute networks of connectivity, opportunities for new applications proliferate. Most consequential is the Internet, whose users already approach 100 million. By 2005 the figure will be 1 billion, and by 2010 half the world's anticipated population of 7 billion will be connected. It is hard to exaggerate, yet impossible to comprehend, how this will change the world.

In addition to the widespread changes in international commerce that constitute globalization, telemedicine is revolutionizing medical practice. Distance learning will dramatically increase access to higher education. The nature of warfare is being transformed by new sensing and targeting technologies. The convergence of television and computer technology is under way with digital set-top boxes and video streaming. As broadcasters begin transmitting digital signals, the convergence will accelerate. The promise of the new information technologies, as Frances Cairncross writes in *The Death of Distance*, is "to increase understanding, foster tolerance, and ultimately promote worldwide peace."[10]

> The technologies have new capacities; they change the way that decisions are made. The challenge is to figure out what the impact is and what that means for policymaking and implementation.
> —Richard H. Solomon

What else will technology offer that will shape the conduct of diplomacy? Collaborative software such as Lotus Notes and GroupWise is widely used by corporations to shrink distance between locations. Videoconferencing, as the technology improves and costs shrink, will become an essential tool for decisionmaking across time zones. Low Earth-orbiting satellites (LEOS) promise the global equivalent of cellular service, beginning with voice telephony to be offered by Iridium Technologies in late 1998 through a network of 66 satellites. US WEST is beginning to offer variable digital subscriber lines (VDSL) to provide high-speed Internet connections and television programs over traditional copper telephone lines.

> One has to make the assumption that we now live in a kind of completely transparent world, that everything will be possibly known by everyone.
> —Peter Schwartz

Search engines such as AltaVista and Lycos are becoming more effective at locating material on the Web. And intelligent agents, sometimes called knowbots, promise to be even better in locating and aggregating customized information. Personal digital assistants are substituting for secretaries by complementing cellular phones and pagers for

---

8. Ibid., 21.
9. Ibid., 17.
10. Frances Cairncross, *The Death of Distance* (Boston: Harvard Business School Press, 1997), xvi.

people who must conduct business outside of their offices. Indeed, by abandoning wired offices, knowledge workers are shrinking distance to stay closer to their clients.

Computers can recognize not only handwriting but also voice commands. Still imperfect, several programs are nonetheless attracting attention with their ability to take dictation. Computer translation for Roman-character languages can be done with a variety of inexpensive commercial programs. Although they lack the sophistication of human translators, they serve as a tool to scan inexpensively reams of materials that might not otherwise be seen. Machine translation for Chinese and Arabic is under development.

> By the marvels of modern telecommunications, C⁴I and the military, we have the ability to have a multitude of sensors in the sky, or human intelligence, coming together in relational databases in which analysis can be done faster than ever before.
>
> —Edward Sheridan

If diplomacy is concerned in part with geography, the new technologies provide the means for precision. Electronic identification tags are appearing everywhere, from automobiles to sneakers, from the family pet to laptop computers. The Global Positioning Satellite (GPS) system can be used to identify the location of people and objects. Spy satellites are said to provide a resolution as detailed as a few inches. Through virtual reality, three-dimensional landscapes can be moved to the conference room, as illustrated during the negotiation of the Dayton Accords.

Backed by 30 international telecommunications providers, Project Oxygen will provide additional Internet and video access to 175 countries by 2003 through undersea fiber-optic cable. A recent breakthrough by Lucent Technologies will allow all of today's global Internet traffic to be carried on a single fiber simultaneously.[11] LSI Logic announced a new technology that will have 223 million transistors on a single computer chip. It will allow the integration of several functions in one system, such as a set-top box, a digital versatile disk (DVD) player, and a video cassette recorder (VCR).[12] The industry is on its way to its goal of building chips with a billion transistors by 2010.

> With human rights activists using videocam recorders to demonstrate graphically what's going on in a country, you can't get away with anything. It's harder for people who are abusing people to get away with it.
>
> —Patricia Diaz Dennis

More and faster does not mean better. From DARPA[13] to Xerox, from Berkeley to MIT, researchers are examining how information is retrieved and displayed to make it more accessible to decisionmakers. Solutions include graphical displays called cone trees and perspective walls.[14] The Clinton administration has funded the development of Internet II at speeds manyfold greater than the current Internet. Neil Stephenson's virtual world[15] may not yet be manifest, although imagination and reality are converging as

---

11. Mike Mills, "Undersea Cables Carry Growing Rivers of Data," *Washington Post*, March 9, 1998.

12. "LSI Logic to Introduce New Chip Technology," Reuters, March 23, 1998.

13. Defense Advanced Research Projects Agency of the U.S. Department of Defense

14. "Solutions to Technologists' Top 5 List Will Drive Technology in Next Century," *Washington Post*, December 21, 1997.

15. Neil Stephenson, *Snow Crash* (New York: Bantam, 1992).

institutions like Massachusetts Institute of Technology (MIT) conduct research on integrated electronic devices called bodynets, as gamers and trainers enhance three-dimensional virtual reality, and as electronic noses and microcameras emerge from U.S. laboratories.[16]

> There was a specter at one time, the Orwellian specter, that the use of what we call IT would allow big brother, or the State, to fine tune control of society. What has happened is just the reverse.
>
> —Alan K. Henrikson

Novelist Mark Helprin describes the world that might emerge from the convergence of the new technologies. As a traveler on your way to Indonesia in the next century, he writes, you will carry with you a "slim leather-bound portfolio [with] an uplink that gives you access to everything ever published—a dual-language text of Marcus Aurelius or the latest paper in Malay on particle acceleration. Your reading can be interrupted by the appearance of a friend in your portfolio, a look at the actual weather in Jakarta, a film clip of Lyndon Johnson's inaugural or, for that matter, anything...."[17] Many readers will be astonished if he is right. The Nintendo generation will be disappointed if he is wrong.

Information technology is changing our lives, our society, our institutions, our culture. Yet there remain many constants, including time and human relations. Traditionalists who insist that diplomacy need not change are wrong. So, too, are those who insist that it must change completely. Finding the intersection that honors the past and respects the future is the challenge.

New Media

Contemporary diplomatic practices were honed in an era when the U.S. press was perceived as a means to amplify the government's version of international news. Edward R. Murrow's reports from London during World War II supported the U.S. conduct of the war. That all changed three decades later when Walter Cronkite's reports suggested that U.S. policy was wrong in Vietnam. The U.S. public came to understand that the government and the media had two contradictory versions of the truth, and its trust in each institution declined.

As more people came to depend on television for their understanding of the world,

> When you turn on the nightly news now you hear about Marv Albert in the lead story rather than the World Bank meeting in Hong Kong.
>
> —Richard Burt

market forces drove those who sought mass audiences to reduce their international coverage. For example, former Agence France-Presse chairman Claude Moisy reports that international coverage on the U.S. networks CBS, NBC, and ABC declined from more than 40 percent of total news time in the 1970s to less than 15 percent by 1995.[18] Reflecting the same trend, the proportion of *Time* magazine covers on foreign affairs dropped from 21 per cent to 6 percent during the past 20 years.[19]

16. Michael Dertouzos, *What Will Be: How the New World of Information Will Change Our Lives* (New York: HarperEdge, 1997).

17. Mark Helprin, "The Acceleration of Tranquility," *Forbes, ASAP* (December 2, 1996).

18. Claude Moisy, "Myths of the Global Information Village," *Foreign Policy* (Summer 1997): 82.

Ted Turner's Cable News Network (CNN) sought to fill the gap as international news coverage by the major U.S. media became more sporadic. Broadcasting from Baghdad during the Gulf War was its defining moment, the time after which the "CNN effect" entered our vocabulary. As some commentators began to assume that the media were making U.S. foreign policy, policymakers felt the impact. Madeleine Albright told the Senate Committee on Foreign Relations that "television's ability to bring graphic images of pain and outrage into our living rooms has heightened the pressure both for immediate engagement in areas of international crisis and immediate disengagement when events do not go according to plan."[20]

However, the CNN effect is less powerful than many commentators have assumed. Although the media can be a force in decisionmaking, the media's role is minimal when policy is clearly formed, articulated, and supported. *Washington Times* White House correspondent Warren Strobel, in *Late-Breaking Foreign Policy*, noting the tendency for the foreign policy bureaucracy to disregard the news media, concluded that the media do not drive policy decisions even though "televised images of innocents' suffering can be a factor in moving policy."[21] The media, he argues, take their cue from the government, Congress, and relief organizations.[22] Foreign editor of *USA Today*, Johanna Neuman, in *Lights, Camera, War* found that leadership, not media images, drives policy.[23] The British Broadcasting Corporation's Nik Gowing, in a study for the Carnegie Commission on Preventing Deadly Violence, reports that decisionmakers, instead of reacting impulsively to media images, "treat what they see or read with considerable caution, if not skepticism." He states that the media's role in conflict prevention is "ambiguous, unclear, and often misconstrued."[24]

Because television is so effective, diplomacy has to pay even more attention to those things which are not televisable—the things which are not public cataclysms. Those other things will be the more important, slow, and pernicious threats.

—Charles A. Schmitz

Political scientist Jonathan Mermin, responding to popular sentiment and informed opinion such as George Kennan's view that U.S. policy is "controlled by popular emotional impulses, and particularly ones provoked by the commercial television industry,"[25] found little justification for such conclusions. "If television inspired American intervention in Somalia, it did so under the influence of government actors...who made considerable efforts to publicize events in Somalia, interpret them as constituting a crisis, and encourage a U.S. response."[26] Scholars Steven Livingston and Todd Eachus agree that the U.S. decision to intervene in Somalia "was the result

19. Project for Excellence in Journalism, reported in "Brad Pitt Journalism," *Washington Post,* March 16, 1998.

20. Johanna Neuman, *Lights, Camera, War: Is Media Technology Driving International Politics?* (New York: St. Martin's Press, 1996), 14.

21. Warren P. Strobel, *Late-Breaking Foreign Policy: The News Media's Influence on Peace Operations* (Washington, D.C.: USIP Press, 1997), 162.

22. Ibid., 141.

23. Neuman, *Lights, Camera, War.*

24. Nik Gowing, *Media Coverage: Help or Hindrance in Conflict Prevention?* (Washington, D.C.: Carnegie Commission on Preventing Deadly Conflict, September 1997), 3.

25. George F. Kennan, "Somalia, Through a Glass Darkly," *New York Times,* September 30, 1993.

of diplomatic and bureaucratic operations, with news coverage coming in response to those decisions."[27]

The research consensus is clear: the CNN effect has been overstated. Livingston concluded that the several effects of the media are so frequently undifferentiated that clarity has suffered. He cautions us to recognize that "different foreign policy objectives will present different types and levels of sensitivity to different types of media."[28] Policymakers must consider the media but must not be subservient to their role. The media are not blunt instruments of foreign policy but interactive elements in a complex process.

> In foreign policy, I suspect that what the CNN effect does is make people simply much more cautious and sort of rulebound in not wanting to delegate authority and risk screw ups that occur on television.
>
> —Francis Fukuyama

If it is fair to conclude that the CNN effect has been exaggerated, it is also fair to conclude that its specialized global appeal may well be the model for the future. Globalization will lead to an even greater concentration of media ownership, where editorial decisions are influenced by the global market. Examples are plentiful, from Disney's acquisition of ABC to Rupert Murdoch's control of media outlets from Hong Kong and Australia to Los Angeles and London. Nonetheless, specialized media can now enter the international arena through the Internet with far fewer resources than at any past time. The price of entrance is dramatically lower than it has been for publishing or broadcasting. With moderate technological savvy, practically anyone can have an Internet presence. Although it is reasonable to expect that a handful of international corporations will control the major mass media, the specialized media will continue their rapid proliferation. Except for sporadic coverage of wars and disasters, the world depicted by NBC, ABC, and CBS may bear little resemblance to international news coverage by the emerging media.

> The Internet is an opportunity to increase the news flow, increase the information flow, and to bring more facts and opinions to the table and that, at a minimum, is extraordinary.
>
> —Merrill Brown

Technology, including the convergence of television and computers, will hasten media specialization. The Web sites that provide audio and video on demand will become tomorrow's primary source of news and information. MSNBC Online is already averaging 300,000 users each day.[29] According to the Pew Research Center, 36 million Americans are reading news on the Internet at least once a week, a threefold increase in two years.[30] On the other hand, the audience for cable news is shrinking,

---

26. Jonathan Mermin, "Television News and American Intervention in Somalia: The Myth of a Media-Driven Foreign Policy," *Political Science Quarterly* 112, no. 3 (1997): 386.

27. Steven Livingston and Todd Eachus, "Humanitarian Crises and U.S. Foreign Policy: Somalia and the CNN Effect Reconsidered," *Political Communication* 12 (1995): 413.

28. Steven Livingston, "Clarifying the CNN Effect: An Examination of Media Effects According to Type of Military Intervention," Research paper R-18 (Cambridge, Mass.: Harvard University, Joan Shorenstein Center on the Press, Politics and Public Policy, John F. Kennedy School of Government, June 1997): 1.

29. Merrill Brown, "The Future of News in the Information Age" (speech at the University of Southern California, Los Angeles, April 7, 1998).

30. "Internet Use for News Triples in Two Years," Reuters, June 8, 1998.

with CNN claiming daily viewers in only 321,000 households.[31] As the costs of bandwidth continue to fall, viewers around the world will choose from hundreds of thousands of Web sites. As each will be equally accessible within several years, the criteria for choice will be technical excellence, content, and trust. Unlike broadcast television or radio, signal strength will not matter.

> We have an opportunity in a mixed media way, whether it is the traditional means of VOA or the new nontraditional means of Internet connectivity, to have a very strong and cost effective program for using information as an element of national policy.
>
> —Richard P. O'Neill

Consumers of the new media, seeking specialized knowledge, will share less with each other. Because their perspectives will be more fragmented, government may find it more difficult to develop a consensus on policy. On the other hand, authoritarian governments will find it more difficult to manipulate publics.

Other future technologies include high-altitude balloons, flying antennas, and a digital global radio network. Sky Station International, headed by former secretary of state Alexander Haig, plans to launch the first of 250 high-tech balloons that would hover 13 miles above the Earth to transmit the Internet, video pictures, and phone calls.[32] By the year 2000, we may also see high altitude long endurance (HALE) electronically powered platforms flying above cities to transmit signals below.[33] Of more immediate interest is the plan by WorldSpace to launch into orbit over Africa a satellite that will provide access to 75 channels of digital-quality music, news, and information.[34]

> The guiding principle for the United States has usually been one of openness, of access on all levels, whether that's access for broadcasting, or that's access in open skies agreements for airlines, or that's access through telecommunications agreements for telephone service.
>
> —Adam Clayton Powell III

What is the future of shortwave radio? Its role today remains essential for communicating with mass populations in Asia and Africa and with countries in crisis. As new technologies decrease in cost, however, the next generation will increasingly turn to the new media. Indeed, as the Internet grows and direct broadcast satellites proliferate, governments will have more channels than ever for international communication. Consequently, the purposes and audiences of shortwave broadcasting will have to be redefined within a generation.

> There is not a wide understanding of the powerful place that U.S. international broadcasting has in helping set the table for diplomatic initiatives.
>
> —Kevin Klose

In summary, international mass communication—through television, radio, and the Internet—will be largely determined by the market. Because the mass media will thrive only by maintaining their mass appeal, television journalism will continue recent trends of marginalizing international news. On the other hand, with the proliferation of channels, international news coverage may well see a resurgence. Governments will have a narrow but key role,

---

31. Paul Farhi, "CNN: No Longer Exactly On Top of the News," *Washington Post*, September 2, 1997.

32. Mike Mills, "Haig Floats A High-Tech Trial Balloon," *Washington Post*, April 13, 1998.

33. Joseph N. Pelton, "Telecommunications for the 21st Century," *Scientific American* (April 1998): 81.

34. Mike Mills, "Ready to Launch a Global Radio Network," *Washington Post*, March 23, 1998.

communicating where the market has not penetrated or on subjects to which the market does not attend. To inform and generate discussion, governments are obliged to go well beyond the 30-second sound bite that often substitutes for information. An informed citizenry needs not only headlines, but context. As the cost of international communication shrinks, the value of imagination and innovation will increase.

Globalization

Globalization is the increased integration of the world's economies through trade, finance, transportation, and information technology. Defined by economic columnist Robert Samuelson as "the worldwide convergence of supply and demand,"[35] it is the subject of frequent commentary in the business press. But the consequences, as profound as they may be for the U.S. economy, remain largely unappreciated by the public and shortchanged by traditional diplomacy.

The flow of goods, capital, and people across international borders represents a resumption of trends that developed at the end of the last century. Then, as now, trade, migration, and capital flows were accelerated by technology. Then, as now, governments could facilitate but not control the exchanges. Recognizing the constraints that globalization places on government, CSIS director of studies Erik Peterson writes:

> The fact is that global economic and financial integration is fundamentally altering the menu of prerogatives and options available to policymakers, and new approaches to managing that altered equation need to be weighed carefully.[36]

The role of commercial diplomacy, in addition to trade promotion, is to level the playing field, negotiate international agreements, and monitor compliance.

Globalization includes or is influenced by several kinds of exchange between nations: human (labor, migration, tourism), trade (goods, services), finance (banking, investment), and knowledge (information, education, entertainment).

Although there are many differences between the ends of the nineteenth and twentieth centuries, the greatest is the role of information, education, and entertainment in the growth of the global economy. It is estimated that more than 50 percent of gross domestic product (GDP) in the major Organization for Economic Cooperation and Development (OECD) economies is knowledge based.[37] The primary source of wealth in the United States has been transformed from manufacturing to services. Developing economies, too, are increasingly driven by the Information Revolution, whether it be manufacturing disk drives in Southeast Asia or writing computer code in Bangalore. The knowledge worker, identified 40 years ago by management guru Peter Drucker, is the key to continuing global prosperity.

It's an interrelated world today. We, in one 24-hour period, transfer more money around the world than our total national budget. All right, with this kind of hard fact, go isolate yourself.

—Max M. Kampelman

35. Robert J. Samuelson, "Globalization on the March," *Washington Post*, October 15, 1997.

36. Erik Peterson, "Surrendering to Markets," *The Washington Quarterly* (Autumn 1995): 112.

37. Candice Stevens, "The Knowledge-Driven Economy," *OECD Observer* (June/July 1996): 6.

The economic preeminence of the United States in the Information Age is a function of its great universities, its telecommunications and computer industries, and its media and entertainment sectors. For example, the U.S. Department of Commerce reports that information technologies have been responsible for more than a quarter of economic growth in the last five years.[38] As U.S. industry has abandoned its rigid command hierarchies and encouraged personal innovation in team-based environments, productivity has soared. Because of the new technologies

> That chunk of money represented by exports, imports, and returns on investment is the equivalent of 31 percent of GNP, which is an enormous number. There was never a time in our modern history when we were more engaged internationally than we are now.
>
> —Ellen L. Frost

and liberalized trade regimes, there has been a resurgence of trade and migration, an explosion in capital flows, and an unprecedented exchange of information among countries. Although economists do not have adequate measures of information flows and intellectual capital, it is axiomatic that they will increasingly drive the global economy in the next century.

The effects of globalization dwarf past economic discontinuities. The volume of foreign exchange exceeds $1 trillion a day, up from $200 billion in 1986. Three recent banking megamergers[39] illustrate that U.S. banking is planning internationally. As financial consultant Lowell Bryan said, "This is the end of the national game."[40]

Automobiles, computers, and other manufactured products are assembled from parts manufactured in dozens of countries, constituting what former labor secretary Robert Reich has called the global web. By the year 2000 West European companies will control 14 percent of U.S. manufacturing production, and U.S. companies 16 percent of West European production.

Two-thirds of Coca-Cola's $18 billion in sales already comes from 199 other countries. Half of the $5 billion in box-office revenues generated by U.S. films comes from foreign sales. And foreign students contribute $7 billion annually to the U.S. economy.

> The boundaries that divide nations and countries are becoming ever more porous. The truth is, even if the public would prefer it that way, the United States cannot disassociate itself from the dynamics of world affairs.
>
> —James N. Rosenau

The U.S. economy has added 30 million new jobs in the past 15 years as unemployment has bottomed out and inflation has plummeted. China's trading volume with the United States has quadrupled since 1988. The children of those 30 million new job holders are wearing Chinese-manufactured clothes and playing with Chinese toys.

The Commerce Department predicts that Internet commerce will exceed $300 billion by 2002.[41] Industry estimates reach as high as $1 trillion. That electronic commerce will multiply many times in the next few years is undisputed.

---

38. U.S. Department of Commerce, *The Emerging Digital Economy* (1998) <www.ecommerce.gov/emerging.htm>.

39. The 1998 mergers combined Citicorp with Travelers, BankAmerica with NationsBank, and Banc One with First Chicago.

40. Jerry Knight, "Banks Now Shift Focus to Global Markets," *Washington Post*, April 14, 1998.

Scenario planners Peter Schwartz and Peter Leyden write that "we are watching the beginnings of a global economic boom on a scale never experienced before."[42] They argue that the global networked economy, driven by innovations in information technology, will continue its surge for at least another two decades.

In his masterful three-volume analysis of the Information Age, Berkeley sociologist Manuel Castells writes:

> My starting point, and I am not alone in this assumption, is that, at the end of the twentieth century, we are living through one of those rare intervals in history. An interval characterized by the transformation of our "material culture" by the works of a new technological paradigm organized around information technologies.[43]

The road ahead will not be without bumps, even some major detours. Globalization also contributes to new economic problems. Witness the economic crisis that began in Southeast Asia. South Korea, the world's eleventh largest economy, saw the won drop in value by 50 percent. The world's fourth most populous country, Indonesia, experienced an even sharper slide. Japan is facing a second year of contraction in its economy. China recognizes that failure to maintain its exchange rate will lead to further destabilizing consequences.

> The new currency goes by different names—cybercash, virtual currency, digital cash, bit bucks, electronic money, or just plain e-money.
>
> —Wilson Dizard Jr.

Many economists and policymakers believe that the economic carnage in Asia would have been even worse if the IMF and the U.S. Department of the Treasury had not acted. And, in hindsight, they wonder why early warning signs were ignored and wish that intervention had been swift enough to prevent, rather than correct, a crisis. Others argue that the corrections, however painful, should have been left to market forces. All agree that better information is required.

The consequences outside of East Asia, both positive and negative, are profound. They reach from the European Union to South America's Mercosur nations, from the Russian Federation to South Africa. The U.S. economy, in danger of overheating, was dampened but at the loss of exports and a sharp decline in the stock market. Economic reforms were threatened in Russia by hyperinflation, a loss of productivity, and a default in debt interest payments.

> Today, if the president goes into the Rose Garden and says something dumb, the cross rate of the dollar will change within 60 seconds. This creates what I call the information standard.
>
> —Walter B. Wriston

If the global economic boom has been largely driven by technology, one might conclude that the role of government is to get out of the way. But the driving technologies—telecommunications, high-speed computers, the Internet—would not have existed if government had played a neutral role. Both in funding basic research

---

41. Department of Commerce, *Emerging Digital Economy*, <www.ecommerce.gov/emerging. htm>.

42. Peter Schwartz and Peter Leyden, "The Long Boom: A History of the Future, 1980–2020," *Wired* (July 1997): 116.

43. Manuel Castells, *The Rise of the Network Society* (Oxford: Blackwell Publishers, 1996), 29.

and in creating a competitive regulatory environment, the government has been essential in fueling the Information Age. With and through international institutions such as the World Bank and the International Monetary Fund (IMF), it can correct systemic excesses. Government must reduce the friction in the international economic system—and wisely and selectively apply it when local excesses threaten international stability.

In a speech to the Council on Foreign Relations in September 1998, President Bill Clinton described the faltering world economy as "the biggest financial challenge facing the world in a half century."[44] Federal Reserve chairman Alan Greenspan, testifying before the Senate Committee on the Budget, urged policymakers "to be especially sensitive to the deepening signs of global distress." He said, "…it is just not credible that the United States, or for that matter Europe, can remain an oasis of prosperity unaffected by a world that is experiencing greatly increased stress."[45]

> The highest priority of our diplomacy should be to ensure the competitiveness of the United States in the world economy. We live in a world where other national governments will go to some lengths in order to turn diplomacy to exactly that overriding purpose.
>
> —Joseph LaPalombara

A key insight into the emerging global economy is offered by Castells who, emphasizing that the reach of the global economy is uneven, stresses that "states must become engaged in fostering development strategies on behalf of their economic constituencies."[46] "What becomes crucial, in the information economy," he writes, "is the complex interaction between historically rooted political institutions and increasingly globalized economic agents."[47] These forces are at play in the resistance of Congress to grant fast track trade negotiating authority to the president. Political institutions that ignore international economic trends will restrict the development of new global markets and impede the growth of business.

Diplomacy—as practiced by the Department of State, the Department of the Treasury, the Department of Commerce, the Office of the U.S. Trade Representative (USTR), and a host of other federal agencies—has a critical stabilizing role in this dynamic global environment. When other nations deny market access or compete unfairly, diplomacy must ensure that the international agreements are honored. And when financial instability threatens, the United States must take the lead to restore order.

Public Dimension

George Soros has pledged $500 million for democracy building in Russia, and Ted Turner has promised $1 billion for United Nations (UN) projects. Jody Williams has received the Nobel Peace Prize for her role in a treaty banning land mines. The

---

44. Bill Clinton (speech at the Council on Foreign Relations, New York, September 14, 1998).

45. Alan Greenspan (testimony before the Senate Committee on the Budget, Washington, D.C., September 23, 1998).

46. Castells, *Rise of the Network Society,* 90.

47. Ibid., 102.

conduct of international relations has expanded well beyond the control of the Department of State.

It is a common perception that Americans have lost interest in foreign affairs.

> It's not possible to have any sustained peacetime foreign policy initiative without public support.
>
> —Olin Robison

Hillary Clinton observed in 1997 during her five-nation tour of the former Soviet Union, "public opinion surveys show Americans at all levels of society just don't pay attention anymore."[48] Representative Lee Hamilton, Democrat of Indiana and ranking minority member of the House Committee on International Relations, attributes the change to the passing of the World War II generation of politicians who "believed things were better when the U.S. led."[49]

Despite the perception of an uninvolved public, poll data from the past several years demonstrate that public opinion is very fluid, sometimes leading, sometimes lagging elite opinion. Furthermore, there is compelling evidence that elite perceptions of public attitudes are seriously misinformed. Elites tend to underestimate the public's support for U.S. engagement abroad, exaggerating the differences that separate them and confusing ignorance for apathy. There appears to be a public willingness to respond positively to leadership on international issues.

Every four years the Chicago Council on Foreign Relations compares elite and public opinions on foreign policy issues. The most recent study, based on data collected in October 1994, found public attitudes to be remarkably stable. "Neither old-

> I have a distinct impression that the American people would like to be more involved in foreign affairs than the polls seem to indicate or, for that matter, than our congressmen indicate.
>
> —Walter R. Roberts

fashioned isolationism nor activist interventionism has captured public interest."[50] What changed from prior polls was the absence of foreign policy concerns from the public's top-ten list of problems facing the country. Foreign policy priorities largely reflected local issues among the public: stopping the flow of illegal drugs, protecting U.S. jobs, and reducing illegal immigration. The one exception was preventing the spread of nuclear weapons. Compared with earlier years, there was a substantial decline in public support for protecting weaker nations against foreign aggression, for promoting and defending human rights in other countries, and for helping to improve the standard of living in less-developed nations. On these issues, elites tended to be even less positive than the public.

In contrast with the Chicago data, the most recent study by the Pew Research Center for the People and the Press shows a divergence of public and elite views.[51] Elite opinion was more upbeat than the general public's (based on a sample of 2,000

48. David Hoffman, "First Lady Voices Disappointment Over Americans' Indifference to World Events," *Washington Post*, November 16, 1997.

49. Steven Pearlstein, "On Trade, U.S. Retreating Into Globalphobia," *Washington Post*, December 8, 1997.

50. *American Public Opinion Report—1995* (Chicago, Ill.: Chicago Council on Foreign Relations, 1995) <http://uicdocs.lib.uic.edu/ccfr/publications/opinion_1995>.

51. Pew Research Center for the People and the Press, *Opinion Leaders Say, Public Differs,* 1998 <http://www.people-press.org/apw2rpt.htm> (January 26, 1998).

Americans polled in September 1997). Whereas, four years earlier, the Pew Center found the public and the elites in lockstep on their sour evaluation of world condi-

tions, elites found more reason for optimism. The views of those members of the general public who were college educated and well informed on foreign affairs, however, approached that of the elites. Mirroring the findings of the Chicago poll, the public in the Pew study gives highest priority to protecting

> The American public is relatively impatient with abstract discussions of foreign policy, but tends to react much more affirmatively once it's presented with a concrete case and a strong argument.
>
> —Alberto Mora

U.S. jobs, followed by preventing nuclear proliferation and stopping drug trafficking. Protecting U.S. energy supplies and safeguarding the global environment were also high on the list.

In the landmark study by the Center for International and Security Studies at the University of Maryland, *The Foreign Policy Gap*, opinion analysts Kull, Destler, and Ramsay reported a growing gap between public opinion and elite perceptions of public

opinion. That is, the study found that elites systematically perceived the public as losing interest in world affairs despite numerous surveys to the contrary. "The key finding of this study is that this perception of the public as wanting to disengage is indeed widespread in the policy community, but that it is not sustained by empirical research, even when

> I think American public opinion when it comes to foreign policy in the post–Cold War era is extraordinarily shallow…. Having lost that anchor in a much deeper sea, we are adrift, and that extends to leadership as well as the public.
>
> —Hodding Carter

skeptical policy practitioners are given the opportunity to propose the poll questions."[52] Members of Congress and their staffs were particularly strong in misinterpreting the public mood, asserting that most Americans want the United States to disengage from its global responsibilities. The study suggests that the perception gap exists because polling data are discounted, vocal minorities have promoted isolationism, and the press has reinforced congressional views.[53] Elite perceptions of public attitudes would appear to be reflective of the shrill views of a vocal minority instead of majority sentiment.

Public opinion does not exist in a vacuum but is developed and nurtured by opinion leaders in the government and press. If Congress and the administration do not lead, it should not be expected that the leadership on international issues will emerge from the public. If there is any surprise, it is that public opinion has remained so stable in the absence of a coherent vision of the U.S. role in the world. A new map of U.S. international interests must be drawn to replace the bipolar map of the Cold War.

Foreign public opinion toward the United States is a far more complex topic. Even friends of the United States express an anger toward our presumptuousness, on the one hand, and our indifference, on the other. Some say that U.S. influence abroad is eroding.

---

52. Stephen Kull, I. M. Destler, and Clay Ramsay, *The Foreign Policy Gap: How Policymakers Misread the Public* (College Park, Md.: The Center for International Security Studies at the University of Maryland, 1997), 172.

53. Ibid., 178–179.

A U.S. Information Agency (USIA) analysis of international press comments highlighted deep dissatisfaction with U.S. leadership.[54] Some chastised the United States for not using its power responsibly, while others saw its behavior as disagreeable and termed it "bullying," "arrogant," and "brash." The United States was faulted for an alleged growth of isolationism; condemned for its sanctions policies; and charged with hypocrisy on human rights, global warming, land mine, and world trade issues.

Although public opinion must be part of the calculus for the conduct of foreign affairs, simple surface measures may not reveal fundamental changes, one of which is the international skills revolution. Members of the Nintendo generation, with skills their grandparents did not have, comprehend the world differently—and are able to interact differently with their peers.

> The policymakers haven't quite caught up to the notion yet that the American public is more patient than it seems, that it's not looking for instantaneous policy decisions. What it's looking for is strength and consistency in our policymakers.
>
> —David R. Gergen

With U.S. public attention riveted on standardized achievement scores, it may come as a surprise to find that cognitive skills have dramatically increased during the past several generations. Research initiated in the 1980s by James Flynn has demonstrated conclusively that IQ scores have increased significantly during the past half century in the industrial world. For example, by examining data from 73 studies, he found a 14-point gain in the United States on standard Wechsler and Binet tests. Psychologists attribute the changes to the complex environment to which people are exposed. UCLA developmental psychologist Patricia Greenfield attributes new cognitive skills to an environment where people play computer games like Tetris.[55]

What does this have to do with international affairs? Plenty, according to international relations theorists James Rosenau and Michael Fagen. In the first phase of a project designed to explore whether individuals are becoming better equipped to play a central role in world affairs, they found compelling evidence of changes over several generations. Their data upheld the hypothesis that individuals have undergone a skills revolution. Among their conclusions is the intriguing idea that the changes "will prove to be part of a growth rate sustained by a satellite-ringed, fiber-optic wired world and, equally crucial, by a continuing trend in which people everywhere are increasingly committed to a democratic, free-market ideology."[56]

> The public has become a much more important player in the process of making daily decisions. That doesn't mean that the public makes the decisions although they are awfully influential. I mean, the purpose of leaders is to lead.
>
> —Lawrence K. Grossman

Governance in the Information Age introduces questions well beyond the scope of this paper: Is representative government threatened? Will leadership be replaced by polling? Will the new technologies be used to manipulate rather than inform?

---

54. USIA Office of Research and Media Reaction, "U.S. Status As Superpower: Good; Should Be Better; Bad and Ugly," Foreign Media Reaction Trends Analysis (January 7, 1998).

55. Trish Hall, "I.Q. Scores Are Up, and Psychologists Wonder Why," *New York Times*, February 24, 1998.

56. James N. Rosenau and W. Michael Fagen, "A New Dynamism in World Politics: Increasingly Skillful Individuals?" *International Studies Quarterly* 41 (1977): 682–683.

Within this landscape of change, the one critical element that binds the government and the public is trust. In a global market of competing voices, in a world on information overload, information alone is a useless commodity. Reliable, trusted interpreters are a requirement. The need for reliable information is as evident in international financial markets as it is for the practice of medicine. The information seeker will turn with confidence to such trusted sources as the *Wall Street Journal* or the National Library of Medicine. But where can one turn for information on international relations? There are numerous sources, but none within the federal government that are sufficiently comprehensive or broadly trusted.

> I think we're in the process of a paradigm shift, a global paradigm shift, as people with common interests find ways to interact with each other and to try to influence policies locally and internationally.
> —Geoffrey Cowan

From the time of the Vietnam buildup through the election of Ronald Reagan, trust in the federal government plummeted.[57] It improved during Reagan's first term but then resumed its fall with the Iran-contra scandal. According to an early 1998 *Washington Post–ABC News* national survey, another reversal has occurred. Still, only 46 percent of Americans expressed positive feelings about the federal government compared with 53 percent who were dissatisfied.[58]

> Somebody said to me the other day, "Well, you know, we don't trust the State Department because their clients are foreign countries, aren't they? They're not really the U.S." So that, of course, led to its own conversation because that's not an accurate statement.
> —Milda K. Hedblom

Even though the trend is encouraging, the majority of Americans still do not trust the federal government. Joseph Nye, the dean of Harvard's Kennedy School, observing that the decline in trust is coincidental with the information revolution, suggests that government will undergo a complex transformation in which governance will be shared with market and nonprofit institutions.[59] Increasingly enabled by new technologies and empowered by new skills, nongovernmental institutions will assume many roles traditionally reserved for government.

> The results of diplomacy have almost universally been public at some point or another. But that, in itself, is not the new phenomenon. The new phenomenon is the immediacy of the resulting public impact.
> —Charles W. Bray

For diplomacy to be effective, it must be backed by a public willing to trust government to act wisely on its behalf. Absent that trust, the circle of diplomacy must be widened to include institutions that have earned greater trust. The foreign affairs community must be, and perceived to be, representative of an engaged public.

57. National Election Studies, "Trust the Federal Government 1958–1996," *The NES Guide to Public Opinion and Electoral Behavior* (Ann Arbor, Mich.: University of Michigan, May 10, 1998) <http://www.umich.edu/~nes/nesguide/toptables/tab5a_1.htm>. Trends are interpreted by summing data on two scales ("Just About Always" and "Most of the Time") from Table A.1.

58. Richard Morin and Claudia Deane, "Poll Shows More Citizens Satisfied With Government," *Washington Post*, January 21, 1998.

59. Joseph S. Nye Jr., "In Government We Don't Trust," *Foreign Policy* (Fall 1997): 110–111.

Issues and Interests

The purpose of diplomacy is to advance the national interest. Although one can produce endless lists of U.S. interests, they tend to fall into three categories: security, prosperity, and humanity. Diplomats should be held accountable for improving U.S. security, enhancing U.S. prosperity, and advancing the human condition. Recent examples in the three categories include international treaties to reduce chemical weapons, multilateral agreements in the World Trade Organization (WTO) to deregulate basic telecommunication services, and humanitarian assistance to nations facing food shortages and civil disorder.

> We have to start with the proposition that the first and foremost obligation of American foreign policy is to protect our national interest and to enhance our national security.
> —David R. Gergen

Security interests have commanded the most attention, particularly in a century that has witnessed the death of 170 million people by violent means[60] and produce weapons capable of destroying the world's population. Although the Soviet Union has disappeared as an immediate threat to U.S. national security, the potential for terrorism by rogue states as well as nonstate actors has substantially increased. Sustaining the peace will require continuing attention to U.S. interests in Asia, Europe, and the Middle East. Regions that contain the explosive potential of North Korea, Iraq, and Kosovo warrant extraordinary diplomatic activity. The bombings of the U.S. embassies in Kenya and Tanzania highlight, in terrifying relief, this challenge.

> The highest priority in any period in history has got to be the security of the United States, so if there's any issue where that comes up, something that could threaten the integrity and safety of Americans, that's the first and most important job.
> —Rita E. Hauser

In his classic book on diplomacy, Sir Harold Nicolson wrote that diplomacy's function is "the management of the relations between independent states by processes of negotiation."[61] Among numerous examples, none better illustrates success in reaching a balance of power than negotiations among the great powers at the 1814 Congress of Vienna. Pursuing the balance among great powers continues to be recognized as a requirement for advancing national interests. For example, a bipartisan study at CSIS identified the need to prevent domination of Europe or Asia by an adversarial power as among America's highest priorities.[62] Consequently, Russia's evolution as a democratic state and China's emergence as a major power warrant particular attention. In *The Grand Chessboard*, Zbigniew Brzezinski argues that "the stability of Eurasia's geopolitical pluralism…would be enhanced by the eventual emergence, perhaps sometime early in the next century, of a Trans-Eurasian Security System" embracing an expanded North Atlantic Treaty Organization (NATO), Russia, China, and Japan.[63]

60. Zbigniew Brzezinski, *Out of Control: Global Turmoil on the Eve of the Twenty-First Century* (New York: Scribner's, 1993), 18.

61. Harold Nicolson, *Diplomacy* (1939; reprint, Washington, D.C.: Georgetown University, Institute for the Study of Diplomacy, 1988), 41.

62. Douglas Johnston, ed., *Foreign Policy into the 21st Century: The U.S. Leadership Challenge* (Washington, D.C.: CSIS, 1996).

Although interests have dominated the conduct of diplomacy during the past five decades because of the threat to national survival, the issues that will dominate the new agenda should be considered as well. CSIS senior fellow Stephen Cambone writes:

> On the one side, we find those who argue that there are compelling issues of human rights, environmental degradation, resource scarcity, and so forth that ought to form the basis of the nation's security policy. On the other side are those who argue that the end of the Cold War did not alter the nature of man or of nations and states and, therefore, it is the nation's interests—defined in terms of military threats and access to labor, capital, and resources—that ought to animate policy."[64]

Interests and issues are not contradictory; they reinforce each other. Just as our vital interests require sustained diplomatic engagement with other nations, so do the issues that transcend national boundaries and alliances. They include democracy and human rights; weapons of mass destruction; terrorism, drugs, and global crime; environmental concerns; population, refugees, and migration; and disease and famine.

> The polarization of the Cold War gave a certain pattern and imposed a certain test on how one dealt with certain kinds of issues and, indeed, it tended to obscure the saliency of certain kinds of issues.
> —Richard M. Moose

None of these is new—but all have greater salience in the Information Age. Democracies flourish with the free flow of information. Human rights violations can be better documented. Information needed for producing weapons of mass destruction is more easily attained. The threat of global crime and terrorism is magnified. Environmental changes are more efficiently monitored. Workers, better informed of opportunities, are more mobile. Disease and famine can be better tracked. In short, the world is more permeable.

Democracy and Human Rights

The international affairs mission statement, prepared by the Department of State in 1997, begins with these words: "The purpose of United States foreign policy is to create a more secure, prosperous and democratic world for the benefit of the American people."[65] In congressional testimony, Assistant Secretary of State John Shattuck said that "our goal is to expand the community of democratic nations so that the world will be better-equipped to confront the dangers and challenges of under-development, conflict, catastrophe, or authoritarian rule."[66] Supporting democracy abroad enjoys strong bipartisan support.

---

63. Zbigniew Brzezinski, *The Grand Chessboard: American Primacy and Its Geostrategic Imperatives* (New York: Basic Books, 1997), 208.

64. Stephen A. Cambone, *A New Structure for National Security Policy Planning* (Washington, D.C.: CSIS, 1998), 3.

65. Department of State, *United States Strategic Plan for International Affairs* (September 1997) <http://www.state.gov/www/global/general_foreign_policy/spia_index.html>.

66. John Shattuck (statement before the House Committee on Appropriations, Subcommittee on Foreign Operations, Export Financing and Related Agencies, Washington, D.C., April 1, 1998).

Human rights, on the other hand, is broad enough to defy an easy consensus. Secretary of State George Shultz, in a speech in Peoria, Illinois, on February 22, 1984, said that "the cause of human rights is at the core of American foreign policy because it is central to America's conception of itself."[67] Declaring the policy practical and tough minded, he recognized the many dilemmas inherent in pursuing human rights as a goal of U.S. foreign policy and asserted the need to encourage those democratic structures that respect human rights. Speaking at a reception marking the anniversary of the Universal Declaration of Human Rights on December 9, 1997, President Clinton reaffirmed human rights as a "central pillar" of U.S. foreign policy.[68] Even though the State Department's annual human rights report focuses worldwide attention on nations that fail to respect human rights, diplomatic attention has been selective.

> The United States is, unlike virtually any other society, one that's created on the basis of an idea. And, to the extent that there's an American national identity, it really has to do with the idea of democracy and the promotion of a certain kind of rule of law.
>
> —Francis Fukuyama

Weapons of Mass Destruction

Nuclear tests by India and Pakistan have directed public attention to the nuclear threat. The specter of chemical and biological weapons has been heightened by Iraq's flaunting of UN inspections. Former Arms Control and Disarmament Agency (ACDA) arms negotiator Thomas Graham claims "we are at perhaps the most dangerous period since the beginning of the nuclear age—with the exception of the Cuban missile crisis."[69] Well before the South Asian tests, several sober commentators had reminded us that the threat has only changed, not disappeared. Former defense secretary James Schlesinger wrote that "preventing nuclear spread both should be—and should be universally seen to be—a preeminent objective of American policy."[70] Political scientist Michael Mandelbaum says, "the major military danger now facing the United States in the post-Soviet world is not a particular country but rather a trend: nuclear proliferation."[71] Strategist Fred Iklé warns that "democracy cannot survive in a highly uncertain world in which a smuggled nuclear bomb might be detonated in Paris or Manhattan."[72]

> The highest priority of all is defending the country—preventing military alliances against us; preventing acts of terrorism, whether they're solitary or state organized; and, most important of all, preventing nuclear terrorism of one sort or another.
>
> —Lloyd N. Cutler

67. George P. Shultz, "Human Rights and the Moral Dimension of U.S. Foreign Policy," reprinted in *The Diplomacy of Human Rights,* ed. David D. Newsom (Washington, D.C.: Georgetown University, Institute for the Study of Diplomacy, 1986), 222.

68. Peter Baker, "Clinton Calls Human Rights a 'Pillar' of Foreign Policy," *Washington Post,* December 10, 1997.

69. Barbara Crossette, "South Asian Arms Race: Reviving Dormant Fears of Nuclear War," *New York Times,* May 29, 1998.

70. James Schlesinger, "Quest for a Post–Cold War Foreign Policy," *Foreign Affairs* (January/February 1993): 23.

71. Michael Mandelbaum, "Lessons of the Next Nuclear War," *Foreign Affairs* (March/April 1995): 22.

Although the NSC's James Steinberg says we have no higher priority,[73] it is not evident that the State Department has given proliferation the attention it was accorded at the height of the Cold War. It is true that in 1997 the administration conducted a successful campaign to gain Senate ratification of the chemical weapons convention and brought public attention to Iraq's biological and chemical threat. Nonetheless, the diplomatic and public attention given to weapons of mass destruction has been less than warranted by the magnitude of the threat. With its unparalleled global responsibility, the U.S. government should assume a more prominent global leadership role.

Terrorism, Drugs, and Global Crime

Terrorist bombings of the U.S. embassies in Nairobi and Dar es Salaam are the latest reminders of terrorism that, with global crime and drug smuggling, constitute an increasing threat to international stability. The global village is spawning a new and powerful class of thugs, from the drug barons of Colombia to the assassins in Afghanistan. The administration is asking for $1.8 billion in emergency spending to improve embassy security; the Department of Justice has increased its presence at U.S. embassies; and the National Drug Control Policy Office has seen its resources augmented.

Speaking at the United Nations, President Clinton described terrorism as "a clear and present danger to tolerant and open societies and innocent people everywhere."[74] Although the threat of terrorism has received increased attention since the 1988 destruction of PanAm 103 over Lockerbie, Scotland, and the 1993 bombing of the World Trade Center in New York City, the August 1998 bombings in East Africa demonstrated again the new dangers in an uncertain world. Even more chilling is the possibility of nuclear terrorism, cited by experts meeting in France who reported the smuggling of weapons-grade nuclear materials.[75]

> We have to think now of logic bombs and Trojan horses and worms and viruses, all as part of a new arsenal in a new geopolitical calculus that enables nonstate, substate, or even individual actors to take on a superpower.
>
> —Arnaud de Borchgrave

Global crime—not yet recognized by the public as a threat comparable with terrorism and illicit drugs—is increasing rapidly as borders become more porous and state authority dissipates. Speaking at the U.S. Naval Academy, President Clinton warned that "intentional attacks against our critical systems already are under way."[76] However, the role for diplomacy in the administration's newly conceived international crime control strategy[77] remains to be defined.

---

72. Fred Charles Iklé, "The Second Coming of the Nuclear Age," *Foreign Affairs* (January/February 1996): 127.

73. James Steinberg (remarks at Carnegie Endowment for International Peace, Washington, D.C., June 9, 1997).

74. Bill Clinton (speech at United Nations General Assembly, N. Y., September 21, 1998).

75. Irwin Arieff, "Experts see nuclear smuggling a global worry," Reuters, September 14, 1998.

76. Bill Clinton (speech at the U.S. Naval Academy, Annapolis, Md., May 22, 1998).

77. Douglas Farah, "Clinton Plan Targets World Crime Threat," *Washington Post*, May 11, 1998.

Environmental Concerns

Secretary of State Warren Christopher announced at Stanford University on April 9, 1996, that environmental issues were "in the mainstream of American foreign policy."[78] He promised that 1997 would be "the most important year for the global environment since the Rio Summit" held in 1992. It was not to be. At the 1997 Kyoto Summit, the administration put forward positions too timid to satisfy the environmental community and too aggressive for the business community. Europe charged the United States with abdicating its leadership role, and the developing nations faulted the United States for asking them to sacrifice their economic future. Even though agreement was reached through skillful negotiation, congressional leaders declared that the treaty would be dead on arrival on Capitol Hill. In 1997, the State Department issued its first annual report on environmental diplomacy and announced the opening of regional environmental centers at U.S. embassies in six countries. Six more centers were opened in 1998. Nonetheless, environmental issues remain on the periphery of U.S. diplomacy.

> There isn't much doubt that we have global warming, that we have changes in the deep oceans, that governments are slowly starting to realize that air transport does not respect national boundaries, and the quality of the air around the globe has deteriorated significantly.
>
> —Ogden Reid

Population, Refugees, and Migration

By 2010, the planet will have 7 billion people competing for land and energy. Although population will have generally stabilized in the West, it will continue to soar in Asia, Africa, and Latin America. Migration could become the issue of the twenty-first century as overcrowding forces the movement of more people across borders. A cursory examination of U.S. and Mexican demographics suggests that large-scale migration to the North—legal or illegal—is inevitable. Moroccan refugees are fleeing to Spain, Algerians to France, Bosnians to Germany, and Albanians to Italy. Kurdish refugees are fleeing Iraq and Turkey. Clashes and competition between religious and ethnic groups continue to force populations from their homelands. As the planet becomes more crowded, as transportation becomes more efficient, and as images of opportunity are communicated across borders, migration will inevitably increase. Whether or not it is orderly will be determined largely by astute planning and skilled diplomacy. Not least among the immediate concerns of U.S. diplomacy are the humanitarian issues that, according to Assistant Secretary of State Julia Taft, "are central to several foreign policy challenges facing the U.S."[79]

> The question of how we all fit on an overpopulated globe and how we allow billions of people who currently live in extreme poverty to develop economically in ways which will not swamp us is going to be the big issue of the next century.
>
> —David Anable

78. Warren Christopher, "American Diplomacy and the Global Environmental Challenges of the 21st Century" (speech at Stanford University, Palo Alto, Calif., April 9, 1996).

79. Julia Taft, "The PRM Quarterly" (n.d.) <www.state.gov/www/global/prm/quarterly.html>.

Disease and Famine

Examples abound of whole populations facing starvation, from Rwanda to the Sudan. Even with the remarkable successes of the World Health Organization and the U.S. Centers for Disease Control and Prevention, there is no reason for complacency when considering the spread of infectious diseases. The toll that the AIDS epidemic will take in Africa is staggering. As economic disparities increase, the effects of disease, too, will be magnified. With a decrease in the budget of the U.S. Agency for International Development (USAID), U.S. diplomacy is hardly prepared to deal with the inevitable crises the world will face in the next decade. Immediate humanitarian concerns may serve as the engine to drive long-term strategies on the issues of disease and famine, which remain on the periphery of U.S. diplomacy.

> It is entirely possible for Doctors Without Frontiers, for example, to take actions in a particular situation which will end up influencing foreign policy either by their actions or by the influence they exercise on our public officials.
>
> —Donald F. McHenry

These several issues have one element in common: they represent not only national but also international interests. Sixty years ago Harold Nicolson wrote that "the development of diplomatic theory in democratic States has been from the conception of exclusive national rights towards a conception of common international interests."[80] Although the pursuit of classical national interests may yield winners and losers, the successful pursuit of international issues can yield winners and winners. It is not a zero-sum game.

It is no coincidence that the State Department's geographical bureaus tend to view the world through the perspective of traditional bilateral interests, while the functional bureaus tend to look at transnational issues. Because of their relative prestige and size, the geographical bureaus continue to dominate decisionmaking. Although there are examples of successful integration, including the European bureau's attention to arms control during the Cold War, the diplomatic attention paid to most issues is dwarfed by the maintenance of bilateral relations in an environment often perceived as a zero-sum game.

Dynamic Stability

The elements of change—information technology, new media, globalization, the public dimension, and global issues—at their most benign will lead to cultural disturbances, which in turn will sustain the conflicting forces of integration and fragmentation.

For diplomacy, all of this means both promise and peril: promise if it respects the changes under way and adapts to the Information Age, peril if it stubbornly holds to the practices of the past.

Irrational exuberance seems to be commonplace as Americans approach the fin de siècle. In 1898, as now, there was one undisputed superpower, imperial Britain. New technologies—telephone, motion pictures, wireless telegraph—were changing the

---

80. Nicolson, *Diplomacy,* 36.

world. Trade was expanding. And the twentieth century held great promise for peace and prosperity.

Although the parallels between that age and this are plentiful, the distinctions are profound. A century ago, the industrial age was approaching maturity and state-to-state relations defined international affairs. Politics, economics, and society could be described by the linear equations of Newtonian physics. Although diplomats feared that the telephone and telegraph might endanger traditional diplomacy, nations discovered there was no substitute for face-to-face contact as the number of diplomats multiplied throughout the world.

> The communication in and out from the periphery into the center is much more dynamic than it has been. Publics count. They count in democracies; they count in would-be democracies; they count in systems that are autocratic or totalitarian.
>
> —Michael Schneider

Today, as a century ago, new technologies are proliferating. But, unlike the technologies of a hundred years ago that facilitated the industrial age, the microchip and telecommunications have created a distinctive new economy where information is a critical element of both process and product.

A vast array of state and nonstate actors is involved in the conduct of international relations. Yet, despite the increasing complexity of relations among states, federal spending on international affairs has been shrinking since 1979.[81] If diplomacy is a quaint vestige of a past age, its loss should not be mourned. On the other hand, if its role in managing relations among states remains critical, the nation should have reason for concern. This study will serve to manifest that concern.

If the nineteenth century can be described by Newtonian physics, then the present age is characterized by quantum physics, systems analysis, and chaos theory as scholars map a world of complex relations. Consider the time when relations between countries were defined by occasional contact between heads of state or their diplomatic designees. Compare that with today's robust relations where tens of thousands of contacts are made simultaneously and instantly. It is not merely a matter of degree but a matter of substantial difference when both the speed and channels of communication increase exponentially. That is what has happened during the past century. The new media create new disturbances. And the international environment remains turbulent.

> More and more, what happens anywhere will matter everywhere. Accordingly, it is in our interest to build a global environment in which our values are widely shared, economies are open, military clashes are constrained, and those who run roughshod over the rights of others are brought to heel.
>
> —Madeleine Albright

Twenty-five years ago, using a sophisticated computer model with numerous feedback loops, a team of MIT scientists sponsored by an international group of industrialists and scientists called the Club of Rome predicted catastrophic global consequences if energy consumption was not severely curtailed. The predictions were wrong because the model overlooked the adaptive nature of any complex system. Surely the international system will surprise us by its resiliency. Nonetheless, history confirms that we cannot leave events to chance when there is an opportunity to influence their outcome positively.

---

81. Brookings Institution and Council on Foreign Relations, *Financing America's Leadership,* task force report (New York: Council on Foreign Relations, 1997), 33.

At a time when international commerce was largely state-to-state and when communication was relatively slow, the tools of diplomacy were appropriate. However, with instantaneous communication and capital movement, the multiplicity of states, and the addition of numerous nonstate actors, classic diplomacy will no longer suffice.

This study does not presume to develop the model of international affairs that will advise the proper conduct of diplomacy in the twenty-first century, but it does suggest that diplomacy must operate more effectively in a world in which the dynamic interplay of interests and issues is recognized. Neither yesterday's diplomatic culture nor its technology will survive in this complex environment. New diplomatic tools and training will be required to buffer the turbulence of change and to ensure dynamic stability.

Several features of this new environment warrant comment.

The first is interactivity. The consequences of seemingly isolated actions are nonlinear and often unpredictable. The best contemporary example is the East Asian currency meltdown that began in Thailand. Few would have predicted that the loss of confidence in the Thai baht would lead to a warning by the Federal Reserve about the dangers of deflation, an expression of security concerns by the White House, and the ensuing threat to the global economy.

> A central effort of any diplomatic establishment, however structured, has to be one that enables it to be confident that it has the information and the analytical capabilities to understand the world in which it operates.
>
> —Anthony C. E. Quainton

The second is speed. Decisionmaking must be accelerated if it is to be effective. Modern technology and best practices must be adopted to ensure that government is a real-time actor in rapidly unfolding international events.

The third is the proliferation of new actors. Although governments are hardly without power, it is broadly shared with business, nongovernmental organizations (NGOs), universities, and interested publics—and amplified by the media.

The fourth is the feedback from the environment that requires a rich flow of relevant and accurate information. Although interconnectivity among elements of the system is presumed, an exchange of information with the system's environment adds additional stability. A system that operates on public trust requires reliable public feedback.

In this complex environment, control is elusive. Small changes have distant and unpredictable consequences. International affairs theorist James Rosenau writes that "the prevailing global turbulence is profoundly nonlinear, uneven in its evolution, uneven in its intensity, uneven in its scope, and uneven in its direction."[82]

> It's no longer only a board game of Diplomacy where you're always maneuvering with armed forces and making and breaking alliances. We are in this for the long term. We need to be building relationships.
>
> —Lloyd S. Etheredge

One way to plan for this uncertain future is through scenario building—not to predict the future but to imagine alternative futures and minimize surprise. Peter Schwartz, who specializes in corporate scenario building, says its rigorous practice helps create the conditions for strategic conversations.[83]

---

82. James N. Rosenau, "Security in a Turbulent World," *Current History* (May 1995): 200.

The two scenarios described below—dynamic stability and global disintegration—represent divergent futures of which many variants are possible. They should be judged not on their predictive power but on their plausibility in terms of what is now known. To avoid the temptation of creating models too far removed from our experiences, we have arbitrarily selected 2010 as the scenario year. It happens as well to be a marker for the Department of Defense (DOD) in its conceptual framework for the future known as *Joint Vision 2010*. This is the year when today's first grader will be entering college, when a freshman senator elected in 1998 will be completing a second term, and when Microsoft will be marketing Windows 10.

The first scenario is identified as a period of dynamic stability. International politics is characterized by close working relationships among governments and numerous nonstate actors that are cooperating effectively to solve urgent global issues. International meetings become routine at all levels. New communications technologies support these daily working relationships and the growth of well-informed public opinion that gives purpose and strength to U.S. foreign policy. The world has an emerging international consensus on Wilsonian principles of world order, including free trade, human rights, democratic values, and the peaceful settlement of disputes. The government and the media will have regained public trust.

> The new reality is that we have a very empowered populace, increasingly more so augmented by the tools of technology and the technological revolution.
>
> —Elaine Chao

In this scenario, the world experiences a period of rising incomes, improving health, widespread literacy, and decreasing violence. World population will have reached nearly 7 billion, with the West representing a decreasing share of the total. Although resource distribution will remain uneven, the North–South asymmetries will begin to dissipate as the urban economies of some of the most populous countries—including China, India, Brazil, and Indonesia—continue to expand. Economic growth will continue to be fueled by innovation and deregulation in telecommunications and the availability of low-cost computers.

Recognition of the need for more knowledge workers in the globalized economy will lead to wholesale changes in education. As Nicholas Negroponte predicted, the most significant transformation of the Information Revolution will be the advancement of primary education in the Third World.[84] Higher education, as well, will have been significantly changed by the new technologies. Harvard president Neil Rudenstine points to the "critical interlock between the structures and processes of the Internet, and the main structures and processes of university teaching and learning" as one of the reasons the Internet is fundamentally different from earlier electronic inventions.[85] Management specialist Peter Drucker insists that the university as we now

---

83. Peter Schwartz, "Afterword: The Value of a Strategic Conversation," in *The Art of the Long View: Planning for the Future in an Uncertain World* (New York: Currency Doubleday, 1995), 219–225.

84. Nicholas Negroponte, "Communicating Bits of Information," interview (1997) <http://www.iridium.com/public/winter/pubvce.html>.

85. Neil Rudenstine, "The Internet Is Changing Higher Education" (remarks at the Harvard Conference on the Internet and Society, Harvard University, Cambridge, Mass., May 29, 1996).

know it will pass into oblivion as the new technologies are adapted to learning. "Thirty years from now the big university campuses will be relics."[86]

Health education and medical treatment will improve by means of the new communication technologies. Life expectancy will continue to increase. Global population increases will decelerate. Communication and genetic technologies will lead to more efficient energy utilization and crop production. There will be unprecedented economic prosperity and global security.

> Since the Berlin wall came down November 9, 1989, political forecasting and economic prognostication have made astrology look respectable.
>
> —Arnaud de Borchgrave

The second scenario is one of global disintegration. Between 1998 and 2010, U.S. leadership, wrongly perceiving a lessening of public interest in international relations, will direct its attention inward. NGOs and corporations, increasingly alienated by the lack of government leadership, will pursue their international objectives independently. A reduced budget and an overloaded State Department will lead to inattention and inaction.

Competitive pressures will encourage the media to sensationalize international conflict and erode opportunities for informed public discussion. A growing minority of people will use new communication technologies to retribalize and rebuild ethnic and religious identities across national boundaries. International financial and economic interdependence will become destabilizing as local problems turn into global emergencies. Weapons of mass destruction will fall into the hands of those who feel they have lost control and are unable to secure their rights.

> It's ultimately not that difficult to make the case to people that instability—in a place that we know about, that we can reach in one way or another—is bad for us. Instability anywhere is never good for the United States.
>
> —Sanford J. Ungar

The convergence of information and entertainment will continue as the major media players extend their global reach. Walter Lippmann's distinction between "the world outside and the pictures in our heads"[87] will become increasingly blurred as images multiply exponentially. In contrast with the dynamic stability of the first scenario, the maelstrom of decline will lead to global disintegration.

The very forces responsible for the Information Age, including the unprecedented speed of global communications, will be able to accelerate the turbulence. The media's power to multiply images and exaggerate reality, used irresponsibly, will be enormously destabilizing. A system built on digital communication and trust will collapse if trust disintegrates.

In describing the unpredictable effects of modest changes, chaos theorists speak of a "sensitive dependence on initial conditions."[88] The Newtonian world of cause and effect will not suffice as a metaphor to explain changes that may occur in a richly connected network. That the global network is increasingly interconnected suggests global

---

86. Robert Lenzner and Stephen S. Johnson, "Peter Drucker—Still the Youngest of Minds," *Forbes* (March 10, 1997) <http://www.forbes.com/forbes/97/0310/5905122a.htm>.

87. Walter Lippmann, *Public Opinion* (1922; reprint, New York: Free Press, 1997), 3–20.

88. James Gleick, *Chaos: Making a New Science* (New York: Penguin Books, 1987).

stability. That stability can be undermined, however, if the flow of information throughout the system is erroneous—that is, if feedback loops exacerbate instead of dampen minor disturbances.

To compensate, the international system must provide timely and accurate information to its numerous interacting parts. At a minimum, there must be a robust information infrastructure and information sources that enjoy a high level of trust. The model developed in the sixteenth century, when the network of relations between states was far less complex, does not suffice today. The sovereign's personal envoy provided both information and trust. The ambassador today provides only a fractional part of the information necessary to maintain relations between states and may be discounted by many, both in and out of government.

CHAPTER 2

The Performance Gap

THE WORLD HAS CHANGED FUNDAMENTALLY. Images and information respect neither time nor borders. Hierarchy is giving way to networking. Openness is crowding out secrecy and exclusivity. The quill-pen world in which modern diplomacy was born no longer exists. Ideas and capital move swiftly and unimpeded across a global network of governments, corporations, and NGOs. In this world of instantaneous information, contemporary diplomacy struggles to sustain its relevance.

We seek here to describe the performance gap by comparing the conduct of diplomacy with its promise. Because there are no rigorous benchmarks for analyzing diplomatic performance, judgments are necessarily subjective but not uninformed. It will be no surprise to practitioners and observers that there are numerous gaps between promise and practice. In some cases, they are profound. In others, they will develop unless current practices are changed. Many of the steps necessary to close these gaps focus on changing the culture of diplomacy.

> Without clear leadership from the bully pulpit of the presidency, I do not see, realistically, how we can reinvigorate the public interest and the public understanding of our stake in a United States that is activist internationally.
>
> —Julia Chang Bloch

Early accounts of diplomacy, from Herodotus to Thucydides, reveal an openness and public involvement that would surprise those who assume that diplomacy has always been conducted in private by diplomats. As historian William Polk observes, its practice in ancient Greece, where citizens were encouraged to participate in deliberations, was even more open than Woodrow Wilson would have wished.[89]

Diplomatic relations of the United States are anchored in the Revolutionary War, when Benjamin Franklin was sent to France to seek assistance against the British. By frequenting the salons of Paris, he became North America's first practitioner of public diplomacy.[90]

> To conduct strong diplomacy, a forward deployed foreign policy establishment—meaning an establishment that relies on the embassy structure with diplomats on the ground—is indispensable.
>
> —Alberto Mora

Thomas Jefferson, the first secretary of state, had a staff of five. Today, the State Department has 22,000 employees. Approximately one-third of them are in the foreign service. Expansion was slow until the twentieth century, when World War I focused attention on the need for professionalism in diplomacy. The U.S. entry into World War II led to further increases, which continued through the Cold War.

---

89. William R. Polk, *Neighbors and Strangers: The Fundamentals of Foreign Affairs* (Chicago: University of Chicago Press, 1997), 234.

90. Ibid., 194.

However, as East–West tensions receded, so too did official U.S. diplomacy. Embassies shrank and consulates closed. Budget projections for the next five years suggest the trend will continue.

Diplomacy is the art of advancing national interests through the sustained exchange of information among nations and peoples. Its purpose is to change attitudes and behavior. It is the practice of state-to-state persuasion.[91] Diplomacy includes activities ranging from secret negotiations to public engagement, including many players, both in and out of government. For clarity, however, the term diplomacy is used in this report to represent the work of the greater community of diplomats and civil servants who work internationally to advance national interests. Their activities are complemented by a broad array of nonstate actors.

> The role of diplomacy is to create understanding and to avoid misunderstanding.
>
> —Leonard H. Marks

Because the Department of State is at the core of the diplomatic enterprise, it is afforded particular attention in the study. That the report gives less attention to other government departments and agencies reflects only their relative sizes. Because of its size and historical role, the State Department must lead the changes that may be required of all. As personnel costs represent 60 percent of State's appropriation, changes that may be warranted in the conduct of diplomacy will most directly affect workforce planning and management.

This study is not about national security or foreign policy per se, but about diplomacy as an instrument of foreign policy. As former secretary of state Henry Kissinger wrote, "Every American foreign policy setback, from Indochina to Somalia, has resulted from the failure to define objectives, to choose means appropriate to these objectives, and to create a public opinion prepared to pay the necessary price over the requisite period of time."[92] The study examines both the means of pursuing objectives and the interaction between policymakers and the public.

> We're the world's only military superpower, the world's economic superpower. Yet our influence around the world is diminished by the fact that we don't have a comparable strength in the field of diplomacy.
>
> —John E. Rielly

This study does not assess the role of diplomacy in addressing these or other international issues during the past year: the economic collapse in East Asia, UN inspections in Iraq, threats to reform in Russia, terrorist bombings in East Africa, or death and destruction in Kosovo.

However, it does argue that the foreign affairs community will be better prepared to deal with comparable issues in the future if U.S. diplomacy is brought to a higher level of readiness. Although many issues cannot be addressed effectively with the tools of diplomacy alone, better information and a better-informed public will provide the means for the conceptual coherence in policy and execution that is needed to sustain U.S. international leadership.

---

91. This definition is drawn in part from Chas. W. Freeman Jr., *The Diplomat's Dictionary*, rev. ed. (Washington, D.C.: USIP Press, 1997).

92. Henry Kissinger, "Limits to What the U.S. Can Do in Bosnia," *Washington Post*, September 22, 1997.

Institutions of Diplomacy

There are dozens of federal departments and agencies involved in the conduct of diplomacy. The Department of State, of course, is most prominent among them and constitutes the largest part of the foreign service. Four other departments and agencies also contribute to the makeup of the foreign service: USAID, USIA, the Department of Agriculture, and the Department of Commerce. The administration's consolidation plan, developed in consultation with the Senate Committee on Foreign Relations, will merge USIA with the State Department. USAID, while maintaining its institutional integrity, will report to the secretary of state.

The foreign service components of the Commerce and Agriculture Departments will remain independent of the State Department. So, too, will representatives of the Departments of Defense, the Treasury, Justice, Energy, Labor, and Transportation, all of whom are present in U.S. embassies. In addition, smaller agencies such as the Drug Enforcement Administration (DEA) and the Environmental Protection Agency (EPA) as well as larger ones, the Central Intelligence Agency (CIA) and the Peace Corps, are totally independent of the State Department. The Peace Corps, hardly an adjunct of traditional diplomacy, has 6,500 volunteers serving in more than 80 countries. The CIA, with a sizable presence as well, serves under cover in embassies throughout the world. Overseas representation by the two exceeds the official U.S. diplomatic presence abroad.

> If we continue to think that diplomacy is an arm of the Executive which feeds information into the executive branch and that's really as far as it goes, we risk a continuation of the erosion of the American public's interest in diplomacy.
> —Charles A. Schmitz

Although the Department of State has the statutory authority for the conduct of foreign relations, its representation in embassies abroad has progressively diminished during the past several decades as a result of budget cuts and the growth of other overseas elements of the federal government. The General Accounting Office (GAO) found that in the decade from 1984 to 1994, the number of foreign service officers serving in U.S. embassies declined from 63 percent to 53 percent of the U.S. workforce in those locations.[93] The trend has continued through 1998. The foreign service—representing State, USAID, USIA, Commerce, and Agriculture—now constitutes less than half of the U.S. personnel at U.S. embassies. The State Department increasingly finds itself playing landlord to other federal departments and agencies.

> It is past time that the State Department get over its rivalry with other agencies. Ambassadors ought to be claiming credit for their work rather than almost resenting their presence, an attitude I find quite often.
> —Anthony Lake

Who's in charge? On the surface the answer seems clear. In practice, it is far more complex. Overseas, the ambassador is responsible for coordinating all diplomatic activities in the country of his assignment. In Washington, the president exercises his responsibility through the National Security Council (NSC) and its staff. Created in

---

93. General Accounting Office, *Overseas Presence: Staffing at U.S. Diplomatic Posts,* fact sheet GAO/NSIAD-95-50FS (Washington, D.C.: General Accounting Office, December 28, 1994).

1947 under President Truman, the NSC's function is to advise and assist the president on national security and to coordinate policies among government agencies.

National security advisers, who run the NSC on a day-to-day basis, have ranged from coordinators such as Brent Scowcroft to primary executors of policy such as Henry Kissinger. The frequent restructuring of relations between the NSC and the State Department reflects not only changing conditions but also recurring bureaucratic turf battles. Former secretary of state George Shultz's dramatic account of the breakdown of communication during the Iran-contra fiasco illustrates the difficulty of coordination when policies are not bound by common visions and values.[94]

> The State Department is too layered, it's too hierarchical, and it's a command and control organization. It is the classic Weberian kind of model of a bureaucracy.
>
> —Richard Burt

President Bush issued his first national security directive early in his presidency to clarify the role of the NSC as the principal forum for consideration of national security policy, the body to advise and assist the president in integrating all aspects of national security policy, and the president's principal means for coordinating executive departments and agencies. President Clinton reaffirmed these NSC roles on the day of his inauguration. On security matters, the NSC is the principal body for policymaking and coordination in the federal government.

The future will witness more change and even more proposals for assigning responsibility and simplifying decisionmaking. Because these issues exceed the mandate of this report, it instead addresses the competence of diplomats and civil servants to advise policymakers and execute their policies in an increasingly complex world. That some presidents and secretaries have not effectively used the bureaucracy of diplomacy to advance national interests reflects, in part, their own personal style but also the failure of diplomacy to keep up with the pace of change.

> The foreign policy bureaucracy is an impediment to careful thought much of the time, creative thought most of the time, and to speedy action almost all the time.
>
> —Lawrence S. Eagleburger

To comment on the performance gap, it is appropriate to pose the question: What do diplomats do? The Vienna convention of 1961 on diplomatic and consular relations suggests several functions: represent and protect national interests; negotiate; report and gather information; and promote friendly relations, including economic, cultural, scientific, and commercial interests. Great Britain's former foreign minister Douglas Hurd suggests that the promotion of commercial and cultural relations is increasingly the most important[95] although these are the very activities that those trained in "high diplomacy" avoid. USIA, the Commerce and Agriculture Departments, USTR, and others have been charged with most of these responsibilities.

What of the other functions? Representing and protecting U.S. interests is an indispensable function that is carried out with pride and professionalism. Negotiations

---

94. George Shultz, *Turmoil and Triumph: My Years as Secretary of State* (New York: Scribner's, 1993).

95. Douglas Hurd, "Has Diplomacy a Future?" (Ditchley Foundation Lecture XXXIII, Oxford-shire County, United Kingdom, 1996).

are critical but, with the exception of arms control, human rights, and occasional bilateral issues, they are increasingly the responsibility of agencies other than the State Department. Reporting and gathering information remain a key function of State, but its nature has changed dramatically because of the Information Revolution. Selecting and interpreting information constitute the greater need. Decisionmakers require trusted sources who can assimilate and synthesize information.

What is missing from the list? Program management, brokering, consensus building, facilitation. Craig Johnstone, the State Department's director of resources, plans, and policy, has signaled a paradigm shift in the Department of State. "We do not want to see narcotics flowing into this country. The policy determination process is over. It took a nanosecond. Now what are you going to do about it? How are you going to stop the narcotics? What kind of programs are you going to build to interdict drugs?"[96] In the old days, policies were developed and announced. It was presumed that they would be respected by nations that exercised less power. Today, the emphasis is on coordination and implementation.

Among today's priorities, representing and protecting U.S. interests remain at the head of the list. Otherwise, the old order is reversed. In the new order of importance, the priorities are

- Program management,
- Promotion of national interests,
- Interpreting information,
- Negotiating agreements.

How well does the United States perform? The Department of State takes second place to no foreign ministry from any country in its aggressive protection and representation of national interests. There is a significant gap, however, between the current capabilities and the new priorities of diplomacy. Whereas USAID, USIA, and Commerce have a number of officers expert in all aspects of program management—including planning, implementation, and evaluation—these skills are relatively scarce in the State Department. The promotion of economic and cultural interests has seriously suffered as USIA has closed facilities and withdrawn officers from postings abroad. The Department of Commerce has enjoyed modest increases during the past few years although they are hardly commensurate with the growing opportunities for trade promotion.

> What's missing is the individual who can explain, who can give background, who can point to the errors of, who can be persuasive because he's speaking with a certain degree of authority and reputation known by others.
>
> —David I. Hitchcock

Although U.S. diplomacy in the broadest sense remains robust, the performance gap at the official level is widening. Workforce planning and management have not kept up with the requirements for conducting diplomacy. As a consequence, professionalism is slipping. State, traditionally expert at gathering and reporting information, is less proficient at rapidly selecting and interpreting information useful to policymakers. U.S. negotiators are among the best although negotiating skills are

---

96. Craig Johnstone, "The End of Foreign Policy" (speech at Dacor Bacon House Foundation conference, "World Affairs and Diplomacy in the 21st Century," Washington, D.C., October 3, 1997), 51.

neither systematically taught nor rewarded in the foreign service. High-profile exceptions are not the norm.

The trend appears to be universal. At a 1997 international conference sponsored by Great Britain's Foreign & Commonwealth Office, most of the participants agreed that reform was overdue.[97] One signal of the peril is evident when the definition of profession is examined:

> A calling requiring specialized knowledge and often long and intensive preparation including instructions in skills and methods as well as in the scientific, historical, or scholarly principles underlying such skills and methods, maintaining by force of organization or concerted opinion high standards of achievement and conduct, and committing its members to continued study and to a kind of work that has for its prime purpose the rendering of a public service.[98]

The current foreign service examination, administered by the board of examiners for State and USIA, does not measure specialized knowledge. Long and intensive preparation is not required to enter the diplomatic service. The Foreign Service Institute offers only limited instruction in skills and methods and almost none in the scientific, historical, or scholarly principles of diplomacy. Although high standards are expected, they are enforced through a top-down evaluation system more than through the force of organization or concerted opinion. The sense of mutual respect that professional soldiers, lawyers, or doctors accord each other is woefully lacking in relations among the coterie of officers who are responsible for U.S. diplomacy.

> I would almost always take limited resources and focus them, where possible, on people.
>
> —Olin Robison

In contrast with the general entry requirements for State and USIA, the other three foreign affairs agencies—USAID, Commerce, Agriculture—include a more rigorous assessment of candidates' professional experience and education. It is a model worthy of consideration for the entire foreign service.

To restore professionalism to diplomacy, the first consideration must be specialization. Are diplomats to be geographical dilettantes with a little knowledge about everything? What might qualify one as a contestant on *Jeopardy* is hardly adequate for diplomacy. The value that diplomacy can add to the conduct of international relations comes from country or regional expertise plus functional knowledge. In a complex world, diplomats, like all other professionals, must specialize. On the other hand, specialization should not become an excuse for regional myopia. As officers advance to leadership positions, they must expand their knowledge beyond a single specialty. Just as specialization is required early in a career, so too are

> When we prepare somebody to serve in Russia, there is an enormous waste if that person does not have two or maybe three tours during their career in Russia, and maybe one or two more in the Ukraine or countries where you could draw on a lot of that.
>
> —Stanton H. Burnett

97. Conference on "Diplomacy: Profession in Peril?" sponsored by Foreign & Commonwealth Office, at Wilton Park, Steyning, West Sussex, Great Britain, July 21–25, 1997.

98. *Webster's Third New International Dictionary* (Springfield, Mass.: Merriam-Webster, 1986).

skills of cross-regional and functional integration at the senior levels of the foreign service.

How does the State Department measure up today? The answer is mixed. Although there are extraordinarily accomplished officers who specialize in the Middle East, in Japan, in Germany, and other geographical areas and although language competence is required of all, many officers move from country to country with less than expert regional or functional knowledge. The same is true of USIA officers. Commerce, Agriculture, and USAID require functional specialization although country expertise is spotty.

The role of ambassadors has changed dramatically during the past decade, so much so that last year John Kerr, ambassador from Great Britain, joked in a luncheon address in Washington that he was returning home because there was nothing left to do.[99] As the requirements for classic diplomacy have diminished, however, the demands for managing transnational activities and promoting national interests have sharply increased.

> Ambassadors are more important than they were before. Technological change means that people on the ground are going to have more impact, not less.
>
> —Richard Burt

In his insightful book on an ambassador's changing role in Washington, Ambassador Allan Gotlieb of Canada says, "The new diplomacy, as I call it, is, to a large extent, public diplomacy and requires different skills, techniques, and attitudes than those found in traditional diplomacy."[100]

The nomination and confirmation of U.S. ambassadors is the subject of frequent attention. As a result of much-publicized abuses in the appointment process, including the frequent requirement for sizable campaign contributions, political appointees have been vilified by the media and the career service. Yet those with a distinguished record of public service or relevant expertise number among the most effective U.S. ambassadors, including Averell Harriman, Ellsworth Bunker, Arthur Burns, and Walter Mondale. The fault is not with political ambassadors per se but with political ambassadors who lack the experience and expertise for representing the United States. There should be no room for them in the U.S. diplomatic service.

> "Who are the most effective foreign ambassadors in the United States?" You will find that the ones who communicate well are the ones who have the greatest impact.
>
> —Barry Zorthian

Because of patronage and cronyism, the performance gap is often considerable, occasionally significant. With America's pool of management and communication talent, there is every reason to insist on the highest professional standards. The cost to the conduct of diplomacy is too high to sustain the current system of political patronage.

The ambassador, carefully chosen, requires a staff configured and selected with no less care. The balance between frontline and support personnel, between regional and functional specialists, must be calibrated to serve the national interest. Embassies must be right-sized—reducing some, enlarging others as requirements change.

---

99. Audrey Gillian, "Tony Blair and the 'New Special Relationship'," *Washington Post*, August 11, 1997.

100. Allan Gotlieb, *"I'll Be With You in a Minute, Mr. Ambassador": The Education of a Canadian Diplomat in Washington* (Toronto: University of Toronto Press, 1991), vii.

The foreign affairs community has too many administrators, auditors, communicators, and other support personnel assigned abroad—and too few people who listen, interact, analyze, interpret, and communicate. Diplomacy is too centralized in for-

> It is not central to the purpose of our diplomacy to see how good we are as hotel keepers. There are other ways to do this. There are competent people in most societies from whom you can buy services, either by putting them on your payroll or by contracting out.
> —Anthony C. E. Quainton

tresslike embassies, too light in commercial and media centers. Embassy infrastructure—characterized by imposing physical structures, autonomous agencies, and antiquated communication practices—reflects not only a recognition of the dangerous world in which the United States must operate but also a dwindling resource base. Some support personnel can be reduced by reengineering administrative procedures. Other support requirements can be turned over to resident contractors. There is no reason to ask career foreign service professionals to serve as housing or budget officers, where such services are available locally in the private sector or can be performed from the continental United States.

Effective diplomacy requires more street-smart people in the right places, fewer bureaucrats impeding information and action. It needs a core of cultural-political-economic interpreters, resident abroad, who can mediate between policymakers and publics, who can add value to the gigabits of information that flow between capitals. The need is for interpreters who bridge the chasm between the public and the government by listening and speaking with care. Diplomacy also needs functional specialists—arms control, health, migration, human rights, democracy-building, global crime, drugs, environment, population—most of whom need not be resident abroad. Frequent travel must not be regarded as a luxury but as a less costly alternative to posting families abroad.

Diplomacy has always entailed risk. With the emergence of the United States as the sole superpower, however, its diplomatic establishments are increasingly likely to be targets of those opposed to U.S. values, policies, and presence. The result is a heightened and pervasive risk for U.S. premises and diplomats. The management of that risk, and public acceptance of it, will be a critical challenge for the United States in the years ahead.

The international consulting firm of McKinsey and Company estimates that technology will increase interactive capabilities by a factor of 2 to 5 over the next decade.[101] In other words, those whose professions are built on interactions should significantly increase their productivity. With the exception of innovations in State Department's consular service, there is little evidence that the foreign affairs community has initiated the changes in infrastructure that will keep the profession competitive with other knowledge professions.

These observations apply not only to the Department of State but also to other departments and agencies that are represented in U.S. embassies abroad. Just as the military worries about the tooth-to-tail ratio, so must the numerous departments and agencies resident abroad direct their attention to overhead costs. It must be asked of

101. Patrick Butler, Ted W. Hall, Alistair M. Hanna, Lenny Mendonca, Byron Auguste, James Manyika, Anupam Sahay, "A Revolution in Interaction," *The McKinsey Quarterly*, no. 1 (1997).

each what value is added by their overseas presence—and whether the task cannot be accomplished more efficiently from Washington, or through travel, or by contractors, or by technology. State's ICASS system may be just the tool to instill the necessary discipline.[102]

If the stakes are high and international relations are complex, diplomacy cannot be conducted on the cheap. Yet the foreign affairs community is dead broke. The international affairs budget (the 150 function) for FY 1998 is $19 billion, approximately 1 percent of the federal budget and even less than the intelligence budget. More striking, the international affairs budget is less than one-tenth of the defense budget. Public diplomacy—including broadcasting, academic and professional exchange, and information—costs $1 billion. Is it a valid reflection of U.S. values that the federal government spends 25 times more collecting information (i.e., intelligence) than it does communicating abroad?

> With respect to international affairs the issue is not, I suspect, "shall we spend more money for diplomatic priorities?", but "shall we spend less on traditional defense in order to spend more on new diplomatic priorities?"
>
> —Joseph Duffey

The trends are startling. Compared with the decade of the 1980s, spending on international affairs has fallen 20 percent in real terms.[103] As figure 2.1 shows, federal budget projections prepared by OMB for the next five years show a decrease of another 10 percent in inflation-adjusted terms.[104]

Figure 2.1
Projected Spending on International Affairs

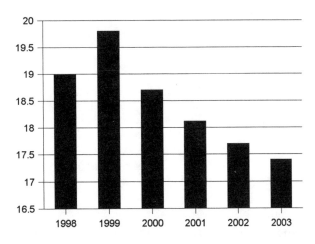

Congress threatens to be even more severe, with a 1999 budget ceiling of $1 billion less than the administration's $20 billion proposal. Secretary of State Albright's success in arresting the decline of resources during her first year appears to have been

102. ICASS, the International Cooperative Administrative Support Services system, went into effect in October 1997 to manage and distribute administrative costs more equitably to all government agencies at diplomatic missions abroad.

103. Brookings Institution and Council on Foreign Relations, *Financing America's Leadership*, 31.

104. Office of Management and Budget (OMB) projects a decrease from $19.0 billion in 1998 to $18.8 billion in 2003 before adjustment for inflation.

reversed.[105] Testifying for the State Department before a Senate task force, Under Secretary for Management Bonnie R. Cohen said, "…the significant decrease in resources allocated to the State Department since the end of the Cold War has left us vulnerable and less prepared to carry out diplomacy in the information age."[106] (See appendix 2 beginning on page 105 for excerpts of the testimony.) With shrinking funds and growing demands, the nation's diplomacy is at risk.

> We had more than a 50 percent cut in our funds for international affairs. That can only be reversed if, in fact, there is a public campaign that creates grassroots support for international engagement.
>
> —David R. Gergen

In summary, there are five related performance gaps that warrant attention: shifting priorities, professionalism, ambassadorial appointments, infrastructure, and resources. Unless the profession is adequately funded and undertakes fundamental changes, diplomacy will be subordinated to technicians and specialists who will lack the cultural and political sensitivity to interact persuasively in a complex world.

Information Technology

It's no secret: the State Department's information technology is obsolete. Madeleine Albright so testified at her confirmation hearings in 1997.[107] Neither computers nor telecommunications networks are adequate. Notwithstanding the tens of millions of dollars spent on infrastructure modernization during the past few years, the task ahead is staggering. In her Senate testimony, Under Secretary Cohen affirmed that "the construction of an information infrastructure to support American diplomacy in the 21st century is one of my most critical and urgent objectives."[108]

> What we have now is just an absolute disaster. The Department of State is one or two generations behind other agencies. It's a real threat to the ability of the foreign service to compete.
>
> —F. A. "Tex" Harris

In an open memo to Warren Christopher a few years ago, technology consultant Joshua Shapiro said "your department is approaching the 21st century equipped with tools barely more sophisticated than when your cabinet position was established in 1789. As one department staffer simply, damningly put it: 'The situation is dismal'."[109]

An internal memo from an embassy in Western European described the consequences:

> It is increasingly, painfully apparent that [the section] cannot effectively support the Ambassador and fulfill its duties in policy formulation and implementation with our current 1970's technology. We're de facto cut off. We do not have access.

105. Thomas W. Lippman, "Albright Calls Foreign Aid Allocation 'Unacceptably Low'," *Washington Post*, June 17, 1998.

106. Bonnie R. Cohen (testimony before the Senate Task Force on Function 150, September 17, 1998).

107. Madeleine Albright (prepared statement before the Senate Committee on Foreign Relations, January 8, 1997).

108. Bonnie R. Cohen (testimony, September 17, 1998).

109. Joshua Shapiro, "Warren Christopher: Read This," *Sky* (September 1995): 22.

It's only going to get worse if we sit still. The world will change whether we like it or not.[110]

A cable from a major capital reports the frustration of a senior diplomat:

> His office now has three PCs which, given the space requirements between the classified and unclassified systems, takes up an enormous amount of work area. Moving from one system to another is awkward and inefficient; it is a waste of time and motion and is a source of great frustration.[111]

In September 1998 the White House added the State Department to the list of seven agencies, including Defense and USAID, that face exceptional problems in complying with Year 2000 computer reprogramming requirements. The Department of State was added to the worry list because it failed to convince OMB officials that it had made sufficient progress during the preceding three months.

Practically every U.S. diplomat, in Washington or abroad, is experiencing information isolation. In recognition of this situation, a capital investment fund to rebuild State's technology infrastructure was augmented in FY 1998 by nearly 300 percent, from $17 million to $64 million. State Department management, OMB, and the Congress have recognized the severity of the problem. Whether the funds are sufficient, however, is questionable.

"Obsolete, dismal, cut off, frustrated." What do these outdated systems mean to the conduct of diplomacy? The first and lesser consequence is inefficiency. Without access to state-of-the-art information technology, it takes longer to get the job done. The second consequence is the denial of information and information-processing capabilities needed for analysis, policy formulation, and communication. The third consequence, even more serious, is conceptual stagnation. The information revolution is changing the relations of nations through the evolving networked economy, the growth of democracies, and increased connectivity among peoples—all of which will remain abstractions to those whose channels are traditional and whose thinking remains linear. Numerous commentators, from Kennedy School dean Joseph Nye and former vice chairman of the Joint Chiefs of Staff William Owens[112] to Goldman Sachs vice chairman Robert Hormats[113] and Novell vice president Daniel Burton,[114] have urged the State Department to recognize the opportunities. Without the requisite technology, diplomacy will surely become an anachronism.

Although most corporations have moved from legacy systems to the Internet or to intranets, the State Department and allied agencies are still operating a secure

> The effect of this new information capability, the globalization of information, has just not been measured and absorbed sufficiently. And I don't see it coming in our younger diplomats.
>
> —Barry Zorthian

---

110. Internal memo from a U.S. embassy in western Europe, 1996.

111. Unclassified embassy cable to the Department of State, April 1997.

112. Joseph S. Nye Jr. and William A. Owens, "America's Information Edge," *Foreign Affairs* (March/April 1996): 20–36.

113. Robert D. Hormats, "Foreign Policy by Internet," *Washington Post*, July 29, 1997.

114. Daniel F. Burton Jr., "The Brave New Wired World," *Foreign Policy* (Spring 1997): 23–37.

proprietary network that is too slow for modern communications. Wang word-processing systems, left over from the 1970s, are still being used in many embassies. Until recently, plans for upgrading would have required three desktop computers for full access to State Department systems.

There is, nonetheless, reason for some optimism. Senior management at the Department of State is totally committed to change. The recently appointed chief information officer (CIO) fully understands the extent of the challenge. The State Department's modernization project, ALMA, is expected to provide embassies and consulates open-systems technology with global network capabilities over the next three years. State has passed the halfway mark in replacing obsolete systems.

> The U.S. government faces a crisis of figuring out how to streamline its own information processing techniques so that they up to date, so that its opinions and decisions are not running behind events that are already well known by the public.
>
> —Sanford J. Ungar

Information resource management has been consolidated. After the completion of Year 2000 corrections and infrastructure modernization, priorities will shift to establishing collaborative systems and databases, offering analytic and presentation tools, and developing a new messaging system. The CIO is working with the Bureau of Diplomatic Security to ensure that the new systems support secure communications.

Despite the considerable work that remains to be done, there are pockets of technological excellence within the State Department, particular in the consular service, which has made great strides in putting complex computer-aided identification systems in place, including machine-readable visa systems and fingerprint-recognition technology. The office of Oceans and International Environmental and Scientific Affairs was an early adopter of the Internet, videoconferencing, and real-time global collaboration in preparation for international negotiations. Political and economic officers, on the other hand, continue to labor with antiquated technology.

Even if telecommunications and computer hardware could be brought to state-of-the-art readiness within the foreign affairs community, the twin hurdles of software and training would remain. The National Foreign Affairs Training Center, recognizing the need, has established the School of Applied Information Technology to instruct both users and systems managers. Constraints of both budget and distance, however, mitigate against rapidly training the professional workforce of the department.

> We have to make sure that more and more of our diplomats are computer literate. Very few of them are. Very few of them understand the technological possibilities in the conduct of diplomacy.
>
> —Arnaud de Borchgrave

Some will argue that training is hardly required for diplomats whose primary usage of the current technology has been drafting cables. To the extent that a Wang terminal has been used as an efficient typewriter, that argument is sound. However, such a view denies the advantages of the analytic, searching, communicating, and networking tools that are now available. As many junior officers in the department recognize, today's technology is at least a generation beyond the diplomatic mind-set of many of their senior colleagues.

Also constrained by budgetary limitations, USAID, USIA, and Commerce have long recognized the need for deploying state-of-the-art information technology. USAID, for example, operates a very small aperture terminal (VSAT) satellite system to facilitate communication between field posts and headquarters. On the other hand, it has invested $100 million in a financial management system that does not work. USIA manages a wideband satellite network for relaying Voice of America (VOA) audio and broadcast-quality video. It routinely uses commercial circuits for digital videoconferencing and made its mark as an innovator on the World Wide Web for communicating with foreign publics in several languages. Unlike their Department of State colleagues, most USIA officers overseas have full access to the Internet and the World Wide Web. The Department of Commerce routinely uses information technology to provide assistance to U.S. business, including virtual trade shows and video-supported "gold key" introductions to investment opportunities. As the cultures of the organizations meld in the anticipated restructuring, it is important to ensure that the agility of the smaller agencies is not constrained by the inertia of the largest.

> We should understand, study, strategize, plan for effective use of information technology. What I think we find ourselves doing is trying to catch up, to run behind it, to react to it.
>
> —Laurie J. Fitz-Pegado

Numerous other technologies in common use in the corporate world are employed only infrequently in the foreign affairs community. They include cell phones, pagers, digital personal assistants, laptops, and videoconferencing. Perceived as luxuries today, they will be necessities tomorrow if diplomats wish to communicate beyond their own circle.

Journalist Robert Kaplan, observing that technology is creating a professional-caste elite in the military, writes that foreign policy will be "increasingly influenced by the military, because war, peacekeeping, famine relief, and the like are becoming too complex for civilian managers."[115] The influence of the State Department has decreased, he says, as the technological revolution has increased the military's clout in Washington.

Two striking examples drawn from diplomatic experiences in Bosnia suggest the future promise of information technology—if it is available to diplomats.

> If we are to take advantage of the massive changes in technology, then we are going to have to find ways to suit the decision-making process to better use of that information.
>
> —Lawrence S. Eagleburger

During the negotiation of the Dayton Accords, computer technology was used by defense analysts to resolve an impasse over the width of the corridor linking Gorazde and Sarajevo. By integrating overhead photographic imagery and terrain elevation information, analysts were able to present to the Serbian negotiators a three-dimensional depiction of the contested space. When the Serbs were offered a virtual flight along the demarcation line, all the while sitting in a conference room in Dayton, the impasse was settled in minutes. Strategic analysts Daniel Kuehl and Martin Libicki report that "the most significant result may have been the imposition of 'information dominance' over the Serbian negotiators.... The American negotiators had in effect said we know where you live and can target it, as you clearly see."[116]

---

115. Robert D. Kaplan, "Fort Leavenworth and the Eclipse of Nationhood," *Atlantic Monthly* (September 1996): 78.

116. Dan Kuehl and Martin Libicki, excerpted from an article for *Jeune Atlantique* (in press).

Another example comes from an operation within Bosnia. At a White House ceremony in December 1997, a team of midlevel intelligence officials was given a prestigious award for the first field trial of an on-site intelligence operation called Support to Diplomatic Operations (SDO). *Washington Post* correspondent Jeffrey Smith reports that Assistant Secretary of State Richard Holbrooke and other State Department officials "worked for months to overcome resistance to the SDO idea at the Defense Department and the CIA."[117] Satellite reconnaissance imagery and other sensitive information provided by this technology are routinely available to military commanders in the field. Smith writes that the disparity between diplomatic and military operations "is felt most keenly when diplomats sent overseas to conduct intensive negotiations cannot draw on up-to-the-minute intelligence, because local embassies lack the gear necessary to send and receive such sensitive information."

> The real dilemma is whether the information technology will be used to ultimately make judgments more reflective or whether it will drive faster and faster decisions, which I think often are not judgment based.
>
> —Stuart J. Thorson

Still another example suggests future diplomatic use. As part of an effort called crisis forecasting, scientists at the Los Alamos National Laboratory are using high-performance computers and new analytic techniques to model complex behavior. Using modeling techniques developed for nuclear weapons design, scientists say "the day is coming when [we] may be able to predict the future of natural events such as forest fires and severe storms or even human events such as political instability and terrorism."[118] The diplomatic community will move further to the margins if such facilities are not available. It is instructive that Los Alamos is spending $500 million for its computer modernization compared with State's $64 million capital fund for a worldwide network.

What is the performance gap? Even if the Department of State maintains a technological edge over most other foreign ministries, compared with corporate practices in the United States the performance gap is vast. State has fallen significantly behind. The proceedings of a conference on American diplomacy in the Information Age, sponsored 10 years ago by the Dacor Bacon House Foundation,[119] might as well have been written today. Well before the end of another decade, the state of State's technology must be dramatically improved.

New Media

Although every element of the federal government has a public affairs arm, the key players in the international arena are USIA and, to a lesser extent, the Department of State. (DOD's public affairs and "psyops" activities are outside of the scope of this

---

117. R. Jeffrey Smith, "High-Tech Unit Kept Watch Over U.S. Monitors in Bosnia," *Washington Post*, December 9, 1997.

118. Earl Lane, "Crisis Forecasting Offers New Ways to Predict Natural or Human Events," *Washington Post*, January 2, 1998.

119. Gifford Malone, ed., *American Diplomacy in the Information Age* (Lanham, Md.: University Press of America, 1991).

study. Likewise, the CIA's past support to indigenous media and clandestine broadcasting has not been considered.)

With the consolidation of USIA and State, there are opportunities for efficiencies of scale as well as risks that USIA's culture of openness will be suppressed. On the other hand, USIA's International Broadcasting Bureau (IBB) will have even more independence that it enjoyed in the past.

Operating under the guidance of the nine-member Board of Governors for the International Broadcasting Bureau (BBG), the VOA (with its new Radio Democracy for Africa), Radio Free Europe/Radio Liberty (RFE/RL), Radio and TV Martí, Radio Free Asia, and Worldnet will not be integrated into the State Department. These services have an FY 1998 appropriation of $386 million plus a $40 million appropriation for transmitter construction. The radio and television services are directed exclusively to audiences abroad through shortwave, AM, and FM— and indirectly though scores of commercial affiliates. Broadcasting in 52 languages, VOA claims an audience of more than 80 million listeners. Adding the surrogates, listenership exceeds 100 million. VOA was one of the first elements of government to use the Internet and now provides both text and audio through the World Wide Web.

> Much of what happened in the twentieth century was predicated on the ability of a few governments to control the flow and use of information. I think those days are gone forever in most societies, and that's good.
>
> —Olin Robison

This study has not attempted to assess the reach or effectiveness of U.S. international broadcasting. The integration of RFE/RL into the IBB has saved hundreds of millions of dollars. The youngest service, Radio Free Asia, has not yet established a track record. TV Martí continues its daily telecasts to Cuba although it has virtually no audience because of jamming. Telecasting to China and Iran by direct broadcast satellite has been cautiously inaugurated. The VOA rightfully takes pride in embracing the spirit of its 1976 charter that mandated that its news be "accurate, objective and comprehensive."

Regarded by some as Cold War relics and by others as critical media of communication, the VOA and its sister services are torn among historic geographical diversity (e.g., the continued importance of shortwave in Africa),

> America's political constituencies— connected by the Internet and by broadband wireless or satellite networks to American television—are now found in all countries. Our "foreign" policy must respond accordingly.
>
> —William B. Garrison Jr.

political imperatives (e.g., the requirement to continue telecasts to Cuba), large capital investments in shortwave radio, and an explosion of new technologies.

VOA and RFE/RL have undoubtedly had a profound effect during the past half century. Although those who did not pay attention to the quality or impact of the broadcasts dismissed them as propaganda, tens of millions of listeners in Eastern and Central Europe and the former Soviet Union found them an indispensable source of accurate information and hope. The research service and archives of RFE/RL were also an important source of information for scholars.

In societies where information continues to be denied, from Iran to Tibet, from Nigeria to Cuba, international broadcasting remains vital and indispensable. For example, recently released Chinese human rights activist Wang Dan told *Washington*

Post columnists and editors that many Chinese listen to the Voice of America and Radio Free Asia because there is no trust in the Chinese media.[120] Wang himself is now contributing weekly commentaries back to his homeland from his new home in the United States.

> I've wanted to steer broadcasting to a closer relationship with the foreign policy agencies rather than a distant relationship. That's a matter of concern.
>
> —Alberto Mora

The question for IBB is whether it will successfully make the transition to the new technologies—to direct satellite broadcasting, to language services on the Internet, to enlarging its network of affiliates. The challenge is daunting, but with annual appropriations totaling more than $400 million and imaginative leadership by the BBG, the successor technologies to shortwave broadcasting can be effectively deployed. Notwithstanding the overall excellence of the news and language services, the performance gap could increase overnight if listeners abandon shortwave for the Internet and direct broadcast satellites. The IBB's early adoption of these technologies needs to be buttressed with a shift of resources as usage patterns change. As the early adopters of new technologies in developing countries are most likely to be in leadership positions in another generation, the IBB must ensure that its media match their interests.

> It may be that our government's greatest function would be to open things up on the other side. If we had a multimedia, privately owned television information system in every country, it would be a good thing for us. And we have a lot to say.
>
> —Lloyd N. Cutler

Practically all departments and agencies of the federal government use the Internet to provide public information through their sites on the World Wide Web. USIA has received recognition for several years for the quality of its international home page. It maintains two sites: one for domestic audiences, largely restricted to exchange programs, and the other, in compliance with the Smith-Mundt legislation prohibiting domestic dissemination, directed at overseas audiences. Of course each site is accessible anywhere. The State Department, which does not labor under such restrictions, offers a single site that provides daily press briefings, the secretary's speeches, policy papers, and country profiles. The USIA overseas Web site—available in several languages—provides a wealth of information about the United States, ranging from the daily *Washington File* (successor to the *Wireless File*) to periodic issues of the *Electronic Journal*.

> I'm willing to more or less accept that there were good reasons for these prohibitions when the Smith-Mundt Act was passed in the late 1940s—but I can say that now it seems to strain credulity to think that this prohibition is still necessary.
>
> —James Schwoch

Each of the sites would profit from better integration and the application of consistently high standards in editorial selection and technical presentation. The State site, for example, instead of being regarded primarily as a tool for dissemination of policy positions, might serve as a forum for the engagement of U.S. citizens. In the aggregate, the sites are ahead of the curve but will require imaginative and technologically sophisticated management if they are to sustain interest. Further, they will have to be perceived as a tool for policy development, not just as an instru-

---

120. Nora Boustany, "Diplomatic Dispatches," *Washington Post*, May 6, 1998.

ment of one-way communication. Feedback can be invited through the Internet in a variety of ways, including on-line discussions and reactions by e-mail.

Although the U.S. government depends on international broadcasting and the Internet for public communication, most publics would remain uninformed without press coverage of U.S. policies. The task of State's public affairs office is to communicate its perspective to the national, regional, and local media—to the *Knoxville News-Sentinel* and the *New York Times*, to PBS and MSNBC. USIA has a similar task with the foreign media that it carries out in nearly every capital.

Does State do its job effectively? Do USIA officers abroad succeed at their task? In both cases, the answer is mixed. Neither has adequate personnel resources to extend its reach to most regional and local media. It is ironic that as more people have come to depend on television for their news, television news in the United States has sacrificed foreign coverage to gain audience share with local

> The federal government has a direct stake in reaching public opinion abroad—a really direct stake, a tangible stake, and it cannot abrogate this role entirely despite its budgetary cost.
>
> —Ellen L. Frost

news. State concentrates its limited resources on the most influential dailies that, however, have readership only among elites in the U.S. heartland. As resources continue to be cut, USIA's access abroad decreases proportionally. It can regain influence in more important, media-rich capitals only if it becomes a unique information resource or plays a carefully defined niche role. The challenge for U.S. embassies is the enhancement of their role as objective, rapid, and reliable sources of in-depth information.

> I would want to strengthen the public communications area of the embassy so that the U.S. message is first formulated clearly, and then it's heard clearly by the local media.
>
> —Edward M. Fouhy

With the proliferation of information sources, the decline of international coverage on U.S. television, and the increased complexity of international issues, it is increasingly difficult for State and USIA to communicate effectively. Nonetheless, because of budget cuts, they have both been forced to reduce the attention they give to communicating with the media. It is unimaginable that they can have the impact they enjoyed when more officers were operating in a less demanding media environment. Despite the best intentions of the State Department and USIA, the performance gap is widening.

It would be a serious oversight to conclude this section without recognizing the impact of U.S. films, music, and the tens of thousands of home pages on the World Wide Web. Despite the excesses of which everyone is aware, the government is decidedly not in the business of balancing the commercial media. Moviegoers here and abroad are not so unsophisticated that the government should feel compelled to compensate for exaggeration, misrepresentation, or bad taste. The First

> I would like to see the media playing a much more positive and creative role in helping the American public understand the really central issues of American foreign policy.
>
> —Joseph Fromm

Amendment is not a slogan but a commitment to the marketplace of ideas.

By innovation and deregulation, the government has encouraged the proliferation of new media. The new international communication environment is one in which democracies can flourish. The risk is that as the noise becomes louder than the message, sound bites will smother dialogue. To avoid this state, the government is obliged to remain active in the marketplace of ideas by providing easy access to information. It is desirable, therefore, that active contacts be maintained with the media, that the new media such as the Internet be artfully utilized, and that traditional media such as shortwave continue to be used in societies where information is denied to citizens. If entertainment crowds out information, the international dialogue will suffer.

Nonstate Actors

The international landscape is crowded with multinational corporations and NGOs that have a direct impact on international relations and, consequently, on the conduct of diplomacy.

> Businesses have little choice but to move to international strategic alliances. Companies like Corning and Toshiba, with more than 100 such alliances with companies across the world, are the forerunners of what will be the rule of international business.
>
> —Erik R. Peterson

There are few U.S. corporations that do not depend on global markets for their growth and survival. The great majority of America's most admired companies, such as General Electric, Microsoft, and Coca-Cola, are household words around the globe.[121] Corporations no longer just move in; they connect with indigenous institutions.

History may mark 1998 as the year of the NGO. Tim Wirth left the State Department to head the United Nations Foundation, established with a $1 billion pledge by Ted Turner. George Soros pledged $300 to $500 million for health, civic, and social programs in Russia over the next three years. And the Nobel Peace Prize was awarded to the International Campaign to Ban Landmines and its coordinator, Jody Williams.

> I would try to make strong bonds with these groups who are working outside the embassy so that my government's policies are carried out, not just by our governmental members but also in concert with the international corporate world, the nonprofit world, and these other outside groups.
>
> —Harriet Mayor Fulbright

More than 15,000 NGOs are directly involved in international affairs.[122] They range from Amnesty International to the International Committee of the Red Cross, from the World Resources Institute to Africare. They include numerous religious organizations such as the World Council of Churches and Catholic Relief Services that enjoy broad public support. Long recognized as international players, NGOs have seldom been accepted as full partners by national governments. The major exceptions are humanitarian relief organizations that can be mobilized before governments can act or when political constraints preclude government intervention.

From Rio to Kyoto, Cairo to Beijing, NGOs have demonstrated their impact in the Information Age. For example, the United Nations Fourth World Conference on Women, held in Beijing in September 1995, brought together government delega-

---

121. "America's Most Admired Companies," *Fortune* (March 2, 1998).
122. *Yearbook of International Organizations*, 34th ed. (Munich: K. G. Saur Verlag, 1997), <www.uia.org>.

tions from 189 countries along with representatives of 4,000 accredited NGOs to finalize a document seeking to improve the lives of women and girls.

How effective are corporations and NGOs in advancing the U.S. international agenda? Their interests tend to be directed at single issues. Unlike the government that, in the national interest, must balance the concerns of competing factions, NGOs and corporations address, albeit with conviction and passion, relatively narrow concerns. On an issue such as global warming, corporations and NGOs often take opposing views. Although corporations would traditionally overwhelm the NGOs by advertising in the mass media, the network of NGOs is becoming increasingly skilled at using the new media, particularly the Internet, to build international coalitions. Grassroots organizers are competing effectively for public attention.

> NGOs in this country, the ones I am familiar with, don't specifically think of turning to the State Department or to diplomats, to assist them in their work. There should be by nature a much more open set of structures in which people function.
>
> —Kevin Klose

Assessing the relationship between the government and nonstate actors depends on expectations, which are in a state of flux. By historical standards, relations between the official diplomatic community and corporate America may be as good as they have ever been. USTR and the Commerce Department, for example, have been aggressive in protecting corporate interests abroad. The Department of Commerce has changed the culture of its foreign service by requiring first-term officers to serve in the United States close to its customers and by introducing objective measures to reward officers for facilitating deliverable commercial transactions. U.S. ambassadors have given more attention to trade promotion. Even with limited resources, the official diplomatic community has focused successfully on facilitating global access to corporate America. A survey of the business community by the Stimson Center shows that the business community has recognized these changes. For example, one respondent said, "…we have noted a dramatic increase and improvement in U.S. embassy support for U.S. firms."[123]

> The truth of the matter is, particularly the NGOs, require a very long incubation of conversation before any meaningful trust is developed for the capacity to really influence them.
>
> —Peter Schwartz

> The mass media, the business community, the NGOs have their own links abroad. If the government hasn't worked out a position and a collaborative relation with these domestic groups, it will be much harder to bring along their counterparts abroad.
>
> —Richard H. Solomon

There is a similar increase in interest in NGOs on the part of the foreign affairs community. The State Department has encouraged participation of U.S. NGOs at the population conference in Cairo, the women's conference in Beijing, and the environmental conference in Kyoto. The scale of involvement is vast compared with the Law of the Sea Conference that began in 1974 or the first review of the Helsinki accords by the Conference on Security and Cooperation in Europe (CSCE) two decades ago.

---

123. *Equipped for the Future: Managing U.S. Foreign Affairs in the 21st Century* (Washington, D.C.: Henry L. Stimson Center, October 1998), 26.

Tim Wirth, on his departure as State's first under secretary for global affairs, compared the new diplomatic challenges with traditional diplomacy surrounded by secrecy:

> The new challenges have to be undertaken in a very different kind of a way. These are challenges that are very public. These are challenges that include a broad base of NGOs—a very different kind of a constituency…. When you think about the difference between negotiating arms control and negotiating climate change, they are two completely different kinds of responsibilities; both very difficult, but the second demanding a significant transition.[124]

The institutional transition from negotiating arms control to negotiating climate change remains to be completed.

In contrast, the Defense Department has shown no reluctance in welcoming the emerging NGO role, particularly those that deal with humanitarian relief. Reflecting on his experience as NATO's supreme allied commander at the outset of NATO peacekeeping in Bosnia, General George Joulwan urged better integration of the NGOs with the Defense Department. To build the team, he said, U.S. policymakers "need to get NGOs and other organizations together with the military."[125]

> State's interests aren't going to be the same as any set of NGO interests, and the NGO interests are only one piece of the mosaic. So, it's going to be a more complicated role for them in that way. You might say they should ride the tiger rather than be eaten by it.
>
> —Milda K. Hedblom

Speaking at the annual Marine Corps Emerald Express symposium, Under Secretary of Defense Walter Slocombe paid thanks to the NGO community for its role in disaster relief. DOD's policy, he said, is to avoid humanitarian disasters through diplomacy and the NGOs. Failing that, the military can provide logistical assistance to other parties such as the NGOs, rather than intervene unilaterally.[126] World Vision president Robert Seiple also called for greater NGO–military collaboration in international crises and said NGO hesitancy about working with the military was changing.[127]

Preparation for the UN-sponsored Convention on Climate Change, which was held in Kyoto in 1997, illustrates the complex environment in which diplomacy now operates. Led by a deputy assistant secretary of state, the U.S. delegation began negotiations with a compromise position that satisfied neither the business nor the NGO community. Critics charged the United States with abdicating its leadership role and either selling out to corporate interests or to the developing world. The U.S. position enjoyed little support in the Congress and none among our allies. The public had little opportunity to be engaged, except to witness the conflicting claims of the corporate

---

124. Timothy E. Wirth (remarks at the U.S. Department of State, Washington, D.C., December 23, 1997).

125. George A. Joulwan (speech at seminar, "Counter-Incitement and the Media," sponsored by The Strategy Group, Washington, D.C., January 21, 1998).

126. Walter Slocombe (speech at Emerald Express '98, sponsored by U.S. Marine Corps, Camp Pendleton, Calif., April 6, 1998).

127. Robert Seiple (remarks at Emerald Express '98, sponsored by U.S. Marine Corps, Camp Pendleton, Calif., April 6, 1998).

and NGO communities. The media amplified the differences. Vice President Al Gore flew to Kyoto to unsnarl the tangle, returning with a compromise that satisfied practically no one. Senate leaders warned the treaty would be dead on arrival.

But the NGO community is no longer without the means to marshal its resources. The rich connectivity of the Internet has opened the possibility of participation on a scale heretofore unimaginable. The land mine treaty would not have been signed without the resources of the Internet and an active network of NGOs. The U.S. government was overshadowed by the rising rhetoric and misrepresented as insensitive to the concerns of the international community.

> More and more, the United States government should take the wise position of trying to partner with identifiable organizations at the national, at the local, the regional, and certainly the transnational level.
>
> —Michael Schneider

Another example of how the influence of the NGOs can be amplified by the Internet is the rout of OECD's Multilateral Agreement on Investment. "This is the first successful Internet campaign by nongovernmental organizations," said one diplomat involved in the negotiations. "It's been very effective." OECD secretary-general Donald Johnson, explaining the diplomatic setback, said "It's clear we needed a strategy on information, communication, and explication." Hundreds of advocacy groups—from the Council of Canadians to the Third World Network—galvanized the opposition that led to its defeat. Canada's trade minister said the lesson he learned was that "civil society" should be engaged much sooner in a negotiating process, instead of governments trying to negotiate around them.[128]

The official diplomatic community and nonstate actors are moving toward a new relationship although neither corporations nor NGOs are satisfied. There is ambivalence about the nature of the change, yet a closer partnership with government appears inevitable if stalemate is to be avoided. It will not be sufficient for government to provide periodic briefings to nonstate actors. The model for the future is more likely to be that represented by negotiations at the International Telecommunications Union, where government and business sit together as genuine partners. The difference is that the NGOs will also be at the table enjoying comparable status. The stakes are high. The outcome is uncertain. But the tools are available for a collaborative relationship to serve the national interest.

Potential for Change

The gaps in diplomatic performance and potential are well known to the members of the foreign affairs community. Indeed, within the past year, the Department of State has begun to upgrade its information technology and has initiated a management study of its workforce. Because such efforts in the past have floundered, many question whether they

> If this is the only institution left in the world which doesn't change while everything else is changing radically, then you are in real trouble.
>
> —Hodding Carter

128. Madelaine Drohan, "How the Net Killed the MAI," *Toronto Globe and Mail*, April 29, 1998 <http://www.nor.com.au/users/ocenia/soundnet/may98/network.html>.

will be sufficiently comprehensive to succeed. It is clear that incremental change will not suffice.

To remain competitive in the face of new global challenges, management specialist Dave Ulrich suggests that organizations conduct an audit that examines their culture, competencies, rewards, governance, work processes, and leadership.[129] To measure its readiness to operate in the next century, 15 members of the American Foreign Service Association (AFSA) were asked to rate the Department of State on the seven scales described in table 2.1.

Table 2.1
AFSA Questionnaire

		To what extent does State have—
A.	Culture	—the right culture to reach its goals?
B.	Competence	—the required knowledge, skills, and abilities?
C.	Consequence	—the appropriate measures, rewards, and incentives?
D.	Governance	—the right organizational structure and internal policies?
E.	Tools	—the right computer and telecommunications systems?
F.	Change Capacity	—the ability to improve work processes, to change, and to learn?
G.	Leadership	—the leadership to achieve its goals?

The average ratings of the group, on a scale of 1 to 10, are shown in figure 2.2.[130] The dimensions with the two highest ratings—competence and leadership—indicate that the potential for change is present.

---

129. David Ulrich, "A New Mandate for Human Resources," *Harvard Business Review* (January-February 1998): 128.

130. Data are from 15 members of AFSA who met on March 24, 1998. The mean ratings are based on a scale of 1 to 10. Although indicative of issues to be confronted in leading change, these data do not necessarily represent the views of the State Department or the foreign affairs community.

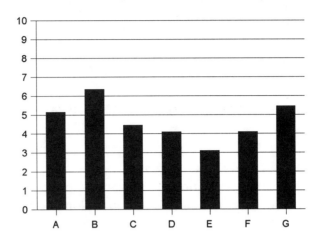

Figure 2.2
Potential for Change at the Department of State

However, the support systems for leading change are deficient. The computer and telecommunications systems rank at the bottom. To succeed, the State Department and other foreign affairs agencies must be agile enough to act effectively within the environment in which they operate.

In summary, there are performance gaps in many areas, including diplomatic priorities, professionalism, ambassadorial appointments, infrastructure, resources, telecommunications, computers, media deployment, media relations, corporate relations, and NGO relations. The administration, the Congress, the foreign affairs community, and the American people must not remain complacent if diplomacy is to sustain its relevance. Without bold action, America's ever shrinking foreign affairs community will be reduced to celebrating its past while others, without coordination or competence, struggle to fulfill the international obligations of the United States.

CHAPTER 3

A Strategy for Change

What Kind of Diplomacy Do We Want in the Twenty-First Century?

THE UNITED STATES HAS A CHOICE: incremental change at the margin or profound change at the center. The first is evolution. The second is revolution. The magnitude of change in the international system and the gaps in diplomatic performance argue for the latter.

In the twenty-first century, diplomacy must be guided by coherence, capability, discipline, and agility. It must be characterized by openness and permeability. To be effective, it must enjoy the trust of the administration, the Congress, and the American people. It must serve in times of both calm and crisis to modulate international turbulence.

> We face an increasingly complex world with very, very different kinds of responsibilities and problems. As a result, we need to strengthen the major areas of our diplomacy, but to do so in conjunction with our assessment of what's required on the ground.
>
> —Thomas Pickering

Getting from here to there is not a stroll in the park. The Pentagon's experience, after years of severe downsizing and new thinking, may be instructive. To prepare for the twenty-first century, it has changed its technology, its force structure, its mission, and its doctrine. Marines are now training as teams, coordinating peacekeeping efforts with NGOs, and learning how to function in an urban environment. Senior officers serve on joint commands to ensure effective coordination across the services.

During the Gulf War, CNN showed the drama of smart bombs and other new technologies. What they could not show was the coordinated strategy among the services that overwhelmed the Iraqi army. Institutional relationships and processes changed along with the technologies. Without such change, new technologies tend to be used for yesterday's tasks. Only when both cultures and technologies grow together can an organization reform outdated practices.

> What the State Department and the U.S. government can do is to facilitate the dynamics of change, maybe to some extent steer them. I guess I would argue for limited goals and more attention to means.
>
> —James N. Rosenau

Some members of our advisory panel said, "Change the culture of diplomacy and the technology will follow." Others insisted that the technology had to come first. We are confident that each must change and that each will change the other in a virtuous cycle of reform and renewal.

Immediately before this project was launched, the administration announced plans to consolidate the Department of State, USIA, and ACDA, and to bring USAID under the direction of the secretary of state. The advisory panel based its recommendations on the assumption that the proposal would be passed into law. Indeed, the omnibus appropriations bill passed by the 105th Congress and signed into law by the president in October 1998 requires consolidation by the end of 1999. The merger should serve to overcome the inertia that has left earlier change recommendations gathering dust in government archives.

The time has come to bring U.S. diplomatic readiness to the standard set by the Pentagon. Without a profound transformation of the tools and techniques of diplomacy, the military services and the intelligence community will have to carry a disproportionate portion of the burden of statecraft.

The advisory panel proposes six strategies for change, each of which includes several interrelated recommendations. In all, they constitute the architecture for transforming the conduct of diplomacy for the first decade of the twenty-first century.

Create a More Accessible Environment

ENDING THE CULTURE OF SECRECY AND EXCLUSIVITY IS A REQUIREMENT FOR DEVELOPING A COLLABORATIVE RELATIONSHIP WITH THE PUBLIC.

The first and highest priority is to end the culture of secrecy and exclusivity, to embrace the notions of openness and trust. The sense that diplomacy takes place in a closed universe of privileged intellectuals must change. Diplomacy must move from a mandarinate system to one that recognizes the permeability of borders and information. Embassies must not become the monasteries of the twenty-first century.

Within this environment of openness, there remains a place for secrets and for secret negotiations. There must be no compromise when national security is at stake. Intelligence methods and sources must be kept from public view. Confidential communications from foreign governments must be protected. Negotiating positions must not be revealed. However, the Cold War habit of shielding the public from information is counterproductive.

> The success of our diplomacy has always depended, and will continue to depend, on its inherent honesty and openness of purpose and on the forthrightness with which it is carried out.
>
> —George F. Kennan

Many of the new issues are poorly addressed by cloaking them in confidentiality. The better the quality of public information about democracy, human rights, environment, population, weapons of mass destruction, global crime, and other international issues, the more effective diplomacy will be. Likewise, the larger the circle of domestic and international support generated by interested citizens, the greater are the chances of success.

The Department of State must engage corporations, NGOs, academics, the media, and the public in a manner that heretofore has been only episodic or excessively precious. We do

> It is the responsibility of the government; the government always ought to listen but not necessarily follow. And I don't like this business of determining foreign policy on the basis of the Gallup poll.
>
> —Max M. Kampelman

not mean a press blitzkrieg to sell policy after it has been made. As the principals would undoubtedly agree, Secretary of State Madeleine Albright appearing with Secretary of Defense William Cohen and Assistant to the President for National Security

Affairs Samuel Berger in the guise of a town meeting broadcast on CNN from Ohio State University to defend positions already reached by the administration[131] is hardly the model for the future. We do mean public involvement in the discussion that precedes decision. The U.S. public needs to know what is at stake when the rupiah falls in Indonesia, when nuclear testing is resumed in India, when fires burn out of control in Mexico.

Leadership

It may be regarded as merely a bromide to say that leadership is required. The secretary of state is first among those who recognize the need. But one secretary does not a revolution make. To effect the changes that are required through the first decade of the next century, Congress, the White House, and the senior ranks of the foreign affairs community must embrace a common vision of public engagement and must pursue it with an uncommon purpose and passion. As a role model, consider Marvin Runyon who in six years moved the U.S. Postal Service from a stodgy, inward-looking bureaucratic survivor to a progressive institution with improved customer service and profitability. He succeeded by putting together a team of like-minded leaders who were united in their passion for change. Success required both risk taking and a conviction that the eventual results would quiet the criticism. The senior levels of the Department of State and other agencies engaged in international relations must insist on developing public awareness and public participation.

> I think that diplomats should welcome sunshine. They should not feel encumbered by truth being known. And I think Madeleine Albright, in some of her own pronouncements, has been exemplary in this, by being frank, telling the facts as we know them.
>
> —John D. Lange

Cultural Reform

To call for cultural reform along with bold leadership is to risk paving this report with good intentions. Too often these words are a signal to the bureaucracy for inaction. Yet there are examples of reform that merit attention.

The federal government's largest institution, the Department of Defense, has undergone extraordinary changes in the past decade—in technology, doctrine, mission, strategy, and size. The U.S. Marine Corps, whose history is as proud as any institution, is undergoing fundamental change by training for what it calls a three-block war—acting as peacekeepers in one urban situation, offering humanitarian assistance in another, and, a few blocks away, engaging in combat. In the future, this may be a common operating environment for the marines. The deputy chief of staff, Lt. Gen. Martin Steele, modestly says the "...baseline for the trans-

> State Department officers take in as a mother's milk lesson the overwhelming superiority of the department vis-à-vis every other foreign affairs agency. And it very quickly becomes ingrained in them that they are to treat others with a sort of contempt.
>
> —Alberto Mora

---

131. "An International Town Meeting," Cable News Network, Columbus, Ohio, February 18, 1998.

formation is there."[132] The trick, he suggests, is to get people talking across traditional bureaucratic boundaries. DOD's resident visionary, Andy Marshall, says it is "striking to me how little [the] people at State look into the future,"[133] but, he adds, there is no reason it cannot catch up.

Catching up requires not only breaking down the culture of secrecy and exclusivity at the Department of State but also streamlining bureaucracy and eliminating the culture of professional castes. Insofar as political officers maintain their privileged position within the State Department, change will come slowly. Openness cannot flourish if professionals remain habituated to the restrictive practices of the past.

New Priorities

There is no shortcut to cultural reform and, in government, no bottom line by which to judge success easily. One starting point is to reorder the priorities of diplomacy. If today they are, as we have asserted, fundamentally reversed, then the institution must explicitly recognize the change. If management of international programs and promotion of U.S. interests are among the highest priorities, the institution must change accordingly. If working across bureaucratic boundaries is essential, the institution must require it. Recognition of the new priorities will lead to a reassessment of the diplomatic skills that are required.

Networking

To give meaning to the idea of openness, the Department of State must develop a rich array of professional contacts within and out of government. Networking with professional colleagues should be the rule. Foreign service officers should be expected not only to belong to professional associations and participate in professional meetings but also to make themselves available to consult with corporations, NGOs, academic institutions, and media organizations. Unlike their colleagues of another generation who brought the revealed truth to others, they should both share and learn. The issues are too complex to require anything less than collaborative analysis.

> Now the verb "to network" is standard at Yale School of Organizational Management or the Kennedy School, and people talk instinctively about building international networks, and that is certainly how international public health policy works.
>
> —Lloyd S. Etheredge

Public Opinion

Through contracts with Gallup and other research organizations, USIA designs and conducts public opinion and media research abroad. USIA also reports and interprets polling conducted by other organizations. The Department of State, likewise, reports and interprets domestic public opinion polls. These functions should be consolidated and strengthened. All research reports should be made publicly available as soon as

132. Lt. Gen. Martin Steele, USMC, interview with Barry Fulton, March 30, 1998.
133. Andrew W. Marshall, director of net assessment, U.S. Department of Defense, interview with Barry Fulton, February 13, 1998.

they are completed. (Most USIA research studies are already publicly shared although some are delayed because of perceived political sensitivity.) Sharing current polling data with citizens will not only enliven the public debate but also enhance trust.

> I do not think that there is anything so radically new about the impact of public opinion and of information that it automatically requires a vastly different approach. I think it requires a little bit more backbone on the part of those who are in charge of the foreign policy of the United States.
>
> —Hodding Carter

Furthermore, the research findings should be systematically considered in the formulation of policy. The disconnect between public opinion research and policy formulation must be righted—not to follow blindly but to consider wisely the voices of those who care about the issues of diplomacy.[134] Although policymakers are particularly sensitive to U.S. public opinion, international opinion has seldom been systematically considered since the Eisenhower and Kennedy administrations.

Balancing Security and Openness

The terrorist bombings in 1998 of U.S. embassies in Nairobi and Dar es Salaam dramatically demonstrated that U.S. diplomacy, however defined or changed, cannot function without adequate security and robust intelligence. Terrorism must be neither the cause for retreat nor the rationale for sustaining outdated practices. The dilemma is providing an environment of security that is compatible with the requirements of openness. Without a strategy that honors openness and enhances security, diplomacy will be forced evermore on the defensive. Because physical security and intelligence gathering involve sensitive information and issues that go beyond the purpose of this study, the advisory panel can serve best by urging that the administration and Congress swiftly reach agreement on supplemental funding to protect U.S. lives abroad.

As recommended on page 59, the Department of State should also carry out a comprehensive reassessment of the requirements for official presence abroad with a view to increasing the representation of country and area specialists and reducing the presence of those whose support can be more efficiently provided by e-mail, teleconferencing, and international travel. A forward-looking analysis, conducted in close consultation with U.S. ambassadors, should result in fewer resident Americans to protect as well as stronger official representation where it matters most. The Department of State should also consider dispersing diplomatic activities—both within the capital and to major population centers within the country—to avoid concentrating personnel in a single, easily targeted location. The activities of USAID, Commerce, and Agriculture could easily and safely be located in office facilities outside of the embassy although linked to it by broadband communications. Consular, cultural, and commercial services should continue to be provided in, or expanded to, cities other than the capital. These changes, instead of reducing the U.S. global presence, respond to the new era of openness, decentralization, individual accountability, and communications capabilities for which this report argues.

---

134. David I. Hitchcock Jr., *U.S. Public Diplomacy* (Washington, D.C.: CSIS, 1988), 21.

Adopt a Disciplined Coordination Model for the Conduct of Diplomacy

THE HIERARCHICAL CONTROL MODEL OF THE PAST SHOULD BE REPLACED BY DISTRIBUTED DECISIONMAKING, DELEGATED AUTHORITY, AND BUREAUCRATIC STREAMLINING.

Just as command economies have failed, so will command diplomacy in the absence of a new collaborative model that recognizes the permeable boundaries between Foggy Bottom and a networked world. Implicit in this analysis and discussion are three distinctive diplomatic roles: traditional, public, and commercial. Traditional diplomacy is largely state-to-state and is often conducted behind closed doors. Public diplomacy engages NGOs, academics, media, and interested publics in a dialogue supported by the foreign affairs community. Commercial diplomacy, conducted in support of U.S. business, seeks to level the international playing field and facilitate business across cultures. To succeed in the future, these three roles must be given recognition and resources commensurate with their contribution to the national interest. The conduct of diplomacy should be guided less by procedural standards, more by a discipline bounded by policy and professionalism. Without such discipline, distributed decisionmaking can lead to chaos.

> The greatest concern I would have is simply to make the parts work together and be able to draw on the strengths of each other, support each other, and so forth. If everybody works together, you lift the embassy.
>
> —Anthony S. Harrington

New Paradigm

The new paradigm of U.S. diplomacy must recognize the distinctive roles of the National Security Council, Department of State (with newly integrated USIA functions), Department of Treasury, Department of Commerce, USTR, other federal departments and agencies, Congress, state and local government, international corporations, NGOs, universities, and the media.

Policy is formed by the interaction of these institutions, coordinated by the National Security Council, and articulated by the president. Diplomacy, guided by policy, is formally conducted by the State Department and other elements of the federal government. It is informally conducted by all of the other players—by the city of Dallas and Amnesty International, by Microsoft and the University of Southern California, by the staff of the Senate Committee on Foreign Relations and the editorial page of the *New York Times*.

> I'm not convinced that there's that much thought being given—as opposed to a simple carryover of yesterday's thinking into a very different world where yesterday's thinking, yesterday's institutions, yesterday's priorities may not be appropriate.
>
> —Donald F. McHenry

To illustrate the relations and roles, consider the metaphor of a Japanese pagoda, with its loosely connected levels held together by their movement against a center pillar called a *shinbashira*. The structure's stability comes not from tight connections or rigidity but from the independent movement of the elements restrained by the massive center pillar. To extend the metaphor, the NSC acts as the pillar or *shinbashira* for policy coordination. The State Department plays a comparable role in coordinating the conduct of diplomacy. The roles are distinct but complementary. If policy is clearly and convincingly articulated, the other elements of government will act as part of a stable structure able to weather international turbulence.

Business Plan

A strategy that calls for a "disciplined coordination model" can be satisfied by a business plan. At the initiative of the State Department's Resources, Plans and Policy Office and abetted by the Government Performance and Results Act of 1993, the State Department has taken the first step in giving direction and discipline through its strategic plan. However, a clear distinction must be made between policy goals and diplomatic practice. For example, that a Middle Eastern peace has not yet been achieved is not in itself a measure of the quality of U.S. diplomacy. To underscore this point, it is essential that diplomats not feel constrained to lower their sights when the chances for a policy breakthrough are slight. On the other hand, it is imperative that diplomatic practice be held to the highest standards of excellence.

Among the requirements of any business plan is a means of measurement. The more complex the goal, the more difficult it is to develop valid and reliable measures that distinguish the contributions of the various actors. If, for example, peace is achieved in the Middle East, does that reflect a careful campaign or decades of effort? The plan must adopt wise measures of diplomatic conduct, of the tools and techniques of diplomacy. Planners must avoid the temptation to lower its policy goals by measuring trivial transactions or, conversely, by attributing causality in defiance of common sense.

Stakeholders

One of the first steps in developing a business plan is to recognize the stakeholders. Who cares if diplomacy is effective? Who profits from its excellence? Who suffers from inadequate performance or failure? If the enterprise is inward looking, the answer tends to be narrow. An organization with a broader vision will be more expansive in its answer. As part of the discipline of developing a business plan, the foreign affairs community should collegially identify its primary stakeholders. They will include members of the Senate Committee on Foreign Relations, the House Committee on International Relations, the Council on Foreign Relations, plus thousands of other organizations that have views on how to advance the international interests of the United States.

Constituents

The foreign affairs community must clearly identify its constituents. It will not suffice to say "the American people" although that is correct in the broadest sense. Nor will it do to say "the White House" although that too is correct in a narrow sense. State, Commerce, and others must identify with precision and care those whom they directly serve, including other departments and agencies of the federal government, state and local government, international organizations, corporations, universities, NGOs, media, and U.S. citizens traveling abroad. They must ask what service the foreign affairs community provides to each and must identify what resources are required to provide that service with efficiency and excellence. More difficult but no less essential, the foreign affairs community must solicit systematic feedback to ensure that value is received. The Department of Commerce might serve as a model in view of initiatives taken with the U.S. business community over the past several years to link assistance rendered with commercial transactions.

> If Americans pay more attention to international affairs, there is a dual benefit. One is obviously for us to become more effective global players but then, also, to understand our domestic situation as well as our diverse population base.
>
> —Elaine Chao

Executive Order 12862 required all departments to set customer service standards; therefore somewhere in the State Department and other agencies this exercise has already been completed. Nonetheless, it should be repeated with broad participation to establish practical parameters for the conduct of diplomacy.

Frontline Diplomacy

One consequence of a practical business plan is the ability to distinguish those who provide services that benefit stakeholders and serve customers from those who service the providers. The military calls this the tooth-to-tail ratio. How large an infrastructure is necessary to support the conduct of diplomacy? How many housing officers, voucher examiners, and accountants are necessary to support a diplomat involved in traditional, public, or commercial diplomacy? With the use of modern technology and management, the ratio can be improved.

The State Department should carefully examine infrastructure and administrative costs with the idea of enhancing diplomatic capability by substantially reducing the size of the U.S. support staff abroad while increasing the number of regional and functional experts. Administrative downsizing can be accomplished by local contracting and by relocating some functions (e.g., bookkeeping) to the United States as electronic connectivity improves. Although we have no analytical calculus to offer as a target, we are confident that the ratio of frontline officers to support staff can be considerably improved.

> The present lack of effectiveness in many parts of our foreign affairs structure is, to some significant degree, the result of organizational dysfunction. The way to solve that is to go back to basic missions, goals, and objectives and rethink the way we organize ourselves.
>
> —Richard M. Moose

Decisionmaking within the department must be destratified. Major issues must move rapidly to the top. Conversely, second-tier issues must be considered and acted on at lower levels. Just as embassies should not make policy on key issues, so too embassies should not be expected to seek approval on issues within their competence. Most second-tier bilateral issues need not suffer the delays of multiple clearances. By eliminating unnecessary reviews, more resources can be devoted to frontline diplomacy. Even as some issues warrant faster resolution than they now receive, others deserve extended study and review. Just as there is no place for procrastination and bureaucratic delay, there should be no compulsion in this age of instant communication to act impulsively.

Vision and Values

The risk in giving up control in a vertical organization is that focus and discipline will be lost. The U.S. Strategic Plan for International Affairs is an important step toward preventing that. In addition, the diplomatic community needs a statement of vision and an agreed set of values. Not a mission statement, a vision statement represents a desired future state, an ideal to which the organization can aspire. The values that guide the organization should reflect enduring U.S. values, including freedom, equality, justice, dignity, and openness. To have meaning, the vision and values must be developed collegially and widely shared. In concert with a business plan and the identification of stakeholders and constituents, the State Department can quietly begin the revolution. On the other hand, with a formulaic approach and a good measure of cynicism, skillful bureaucrats can sustain the hierarchical control model that is rendering diplomacy irrelevant.

> We are, for better or for worse, children of a notion of our own exceptionalism. A part of that is myth, but I think that it is attempting to live up to myths that keeps a nation strong and vital and clean in its own terms.
>
> —Hodding Carter

Lead a Renaissance of Professionalism

REPLACING OUTDATED PRACTICES OF WORKFORCE MANAGEMENT, CREATING NEW PROFESSIONAL OPPORTUNITIES, AND MAKING A COMMITMENT TO SUSTAINED PROFESSIONAL DEVELOPMENT ARE REQUIRED TO CHANGE THE EXISTING CULTURE.

The Department of State must assume the leadership in reforming personnel practices, collaborating with Commerce, Agriculture and other departments to ensure that renewal does not stop at Foggy Bottom.

Career Service

The first step is a reexamination of the career service. State has already begun combining political and economic sections in smaller embassies, yet the career paths of economic and political officers remain separate and distinctive. Plans for USIA's integration include the creation of a separate public affairs career path. We urge the Department of State to combine these three so-called cones— political, economic, information—to encourage a more holistic career service. Members of this service would be designated as policy officers. They should be officers who can serve as information interpreters and knowledge integrators, who are broadly knowledgeable about the politics, economics, and culture of the United States and about the region or country in which they serve. To stress the latter, they should be required to specialize by region. Regional and country specialization is the unique value that policy officers can provide.

> You need different people, you need different embassy structures which are focused much more sharply around issues rather than around personnel categories. And you will need an approach which is much more open to conflicting and diverse players in a multimedia and multicultural environment.
>
> —Anthony C. E. Quainton

A few years ago the department considered and rejected the idea of combining the administrative and consular cones into a speciality that would be parallel to the policy officers described above. The plan was scuttled because administrative and consular officers feared they would enjoy second-class status. This is not an unreasonable fear. Still, we urge reconsideration of this plan along with assurances that those with administrative and consular training, in proportion to their numbers, would reach grades and positions of responsibility comparable with the policy officers. There is no room for second-class diplomacy in the future. Those assigned to this new combined function would be designated as management officers.

Hence, the State Department would have two diplomatic clusters: management officers and policy officers. Substantive officer, a designation that is now the informal term of art for a political or economic officer, would be dropped—with the recognition that the diplomatic services require professionalism from both policy and management officers. The size of the career service should be determined in concert with changes that we recommend for the creation of a reserve service (see next subsection) and for professional development (see subsection that begins on page 63).

Reserve Service

The foreign service will be strengthened by routinely tapping outside expertise for noncareer appointments abroad: academics who specialize in a region; executives who will share their business experience; specialists in environment, population, and other issues. USIA's occasional recruitment of senior academics as cultural affairs officers illustrates the wisdom of the approach. Imaginatively administered, such a program keeps a career service from going stale. Consequently, we recommend that the State Department establish and administer a professional reserve service, using its existing statutory authority to make foreign service appointments for up to five years. The advisory panel is aware of the failure of the foreign affairs specialist program established in the 1970s. It is also aware that the authority has been occasionally used for political patronage. On the other hand, the Peace Corps uses the authority to staff its professional positions abroad with no hint of abuse.

The State Department should designate a significant percentage of its overseas positions for time-limited reserve appointments for professionals from outside of government (corporations, NGOs, academe, media) as well as career civil servants who are now assigned to embassies. Recruiting and welcoming reservists for one-time appointments would represent a change from current practices, where outsiders are usually kept at bay. We imagine that foreign service reservists, after serving on active duty, would be offered periodic opportunities to sustain their involvement, including seminars and briefings, both electronic and real.

Further, we urge recruitment for the reserve service up to the mandatory retirement age of 65, with salaries determined by experience and responsibility. We concurrently urge that the selection of junior members of the career service be age

> I would reorient the embassy based on the real needs that the United States has vis-à-vis that country instead of just continuing on with the same huge staff so that embassies are almost impossible to manage.
>
> —Rita E. Hauser

limited. The current practice of recruiting junior officer trainees through age 60 should be abandoned. It is folly to offer career appointments at the bottom rung of the career ladder to people who do not have time to advance to positions of responsibility. The reserve service will provide an opportunity at any age for those with professional credentials.

Virtual Teams

We have proposed policy and management officers augmented by a reserve service to serve better the proposed new priorities, including project management and promotion of national interests. To ensure long-range collaboration, we propose the creation of electronically linked virtual teams whose membership would be certified after they satisfied rigorous criteria for regional or functional competence. Most officers would serve on no more than two regional teams. With the technology that will soon be available, officers could continue to serve after they had physically left the region. They would not only be kept professionally informed of developments in their region of expertise but would be consulted as policies were developed and implemented. Under current practices, regional and functional expertise is often lost when officers are transferred.

Workforce Planning and Management

The State Department must completely overhaul its workforce planning and management, including recruitment, examination, appointments, assignments, and promotions. It may be the only institution in the United States that does not consider an applicant's education or work history before offering an appointment. It is true that there is an exhaustive written test and oral assessment, but the test is little more than a souped-up Scholastic Aptitude Test. The oral assessment process, although administered with the appearance of objectivity, does not assess regional or management expertise. Even if the process produces candidates who are broadly educated, it does not pretend to assess their effectiveness in another culture or their language abilities. What's more, the process is slow and expensive, requiring up to 18 months after a candidate takes the written examination before an offer of employment is made. Consequently, the current process should be scrapped. It should be replaced with a system drawn from best practices in industry in which candidates are recruited against future projected needs. There is no reason that successful candidates could not be offered immediate employment with provisional and limited security clearances.

> I worry that the actual management of individuals in government, which has never been very strong, has gotten worse. People are not rewarded for being good managers; they are rewarded for deals, for making their bosses look good.
>
> —Ellen L. Frost

During a typical career, policy officers should be assigned to no more than two regions. Management officers, whose expertise is not regional, would have broader opportunities for assignment. After a rigorous tenuring process, promotions should be predictable and nearly automatic until one reaches eligibility for joining the senior foreign service. At that stage, promotions should be highly competitive. What we seek to eliminate is the gaming that officers feel compelled to play to remain eligible for promotion. The system should include the means to recognize exceptional service and to weed out the laggards, but the great majority should move predictably through the ranks as they would in any profession.

In recent years, the foreign affairs community has given renewed emphasis to recruiting minority candidates. To represent the United States abroad, the foreign service must be representative of America and reflect its diversity. In their workforce management, the Department of State and other foreign affairs agencies should continue aggressive recruiting among underrepresented populations. Although that may require unconventional initiatives, such as enhanced recruiting among successful Peace Corps volunteers and military officers, no less is warranted.

Implicit in these recommendations is a skills profile for the future. What skills will the foreign service need in 2010? It cannot recruit effectively without identifying them. Such skills must be developed and honed if professionalism is to be renewed. The skills profile will suggest where recruitment should be focused: within schools of foreign service, management, and communication; among people who have served abroad with NGOs, the military, corporations, and the Peace Corps. Communication skills (including language competence), regional expertise, and management skills should be recognized and rewarded in the recruitment process.

Jointness

To change its caste culture, the foreign service must borrow a page from the Defense Department and institute requirements for service across bureaucratic boundaries. Only after the Goldwater-Nichols Act required service for senior military officers in joint commands did service rivalries begin to break down. Exchanges within the foreign affairs community have long been encouraged but remain the exception. We recommend the adoption of common standards for entrance into a common senior foreign service, whose membership would be drawn proportionally from State, USIA, USAID, Commerce, and Agriculture. Service outside of one's parent agency should be a requirement for advancement to this level.

Professional Development

Apart from language training and area studies, the foreign service is offered little opportunity for professional development. The exceptions, such as assignment to the senior seminar or the service colleges, academic years, or Pell grants, are neither widely available nor are they stepping stones to advancement. There is a pervasive sense that once you have passed the entrance examination, everything you need to know can be learned on the job. Such a practice leads to stagnation, to looking backward rather than forward.

> One of my priorities, in terms of our diplomats abroad and the mission they have to fulfill, is education of those diplomats.
> —Ralph P. Davidson

Among the many corporate gurus, MIT's Peter Senge offers a promising perspective on what he calls learning organizations:

> …organizations where people continually expand their capacity to create the results they truly desire, where new and expansive patterns of thinking are

nurtured, where collective aspiration is set free, and where people are continually learning how to learn together.[135]

Utopian to be sure, yet this is the culture that the department must embrace if it is not to be frozen in time, a victim of its own past. It must encourage lifetime learning and develop a workforce that does not spend all of its time reacting to events. To do so, it must offer more professional education, more exchanges out of government, and more rewards for professional growth. Like the military, the State Department must identify clearly its expectations and stop treating professional development as a way to fill an assignment gap. Consideration for promotion into the senior foreign service should be conditional on satisfactorily completing rigorous advanced study in the substance and process of diplomacy.

> The end of the Cold War and the return to normalcy—plus the rapid development of information technology—means that you really have to focus a lot more on giving yourselves a well-organized, dedicated, and directed diplomatic staff that can, in fact, help you make decisions.
>
> —John Kornblum

The knowledge revolution is too fast paced to expect that the education one brings to the foreign service will be sufficient to serve a generation later. Before reaching the senior ranks, diplomats must be afforded the same opportunities for continuing growth as their counterparts in the military and the private sector. And if the collaborative model we propose is to work, these opportunities must include assignments in other government agencies, NGOs, academic institutions, and businesses. Exchanges with other foreign ministries should also be encouraged. This openness will be another step in eliminating the insularity of diplomacy.

Upgrade Information Technology to Corporate Standards

THE ACQUISITION OF NEW TECHNOLOGIES MUST BE GEARED TO SUPPORTING THE KEY PRIORITIES OF DIPLOMACY.

Information technology is not a substitute for human interaction but an enabler of it. As RAND consultant John Arquilla has reminded the Pentagon, "…focusing too closely on technology is a risky, seductive business."[136] Seeking the balance between human and technological resources is the greatest challenge for diplomacy over the next decade. Just as the status quo is unacceptable, so too is a zealous embrace of unstable and complicated technology that leads diplomats away from the societies in which they specialize to the false comfort of a virtual world. Computers are tools for facilitating the business of diplomacy, not instruments for replacing human interaction or judgment. Author Robert Kaplan says he finds more and more U.S. diplomats abroad sitting in front of their computer screens, losing contact with the societies where they are posted.[137] That is the PC myopia that must be avoided. Computers, properly used

---

135. Peter M. Senge, *The Fifth Discipline: The Art and Practice of the Learning Organization* (New York: Doubleday, 1990), 3.

136. John Arquilla, "The 'Velvet' Revolution in Military Affairs," *World Policy Journal* (Winter 1997-1998): 33.

137. Robert Kaplan, interview with Barry Fulton, February 12, 1998.

to facilitate information management, will free officers to engage the culture in which they live.

Information Strategy

If diplomacy deals largely in information and persuasion, the competitive advantage of the foreign affairs community is directly related to the information tools it has at its disposal. Faster computers connected to networks, as outlined below, are part of the requirement for change. No less important, however, is an information strategy that reflects U.S. values and its global leadership in information technology. The rationale for developing a coherent information strategy is not greater efficiency in information processing, even if that is a consequence. The new technologies, quintessentially pro-democratic, will encourage broader global engagement between publics and practitioners, increase tolerance among isolated populations, and provide information from which shared solutions can be developed. Although international relations may well be more complex than in an earlier era, the further democratization of the process reflects America's deepest values. The greater the degree of international transparency, the easier it is to ensure the protection of human rights.

> The ability and the fungibility of the technology and the inexpensive nature of that technology to get to all parts of the globe instantly make people connected in ways and influential in ways we've never seen before.
>
> —Richard P. O'Neill

Telecommunications

The Diplomatic Telecommunications Service provides connectivity abroad for some 50 government agencies, including the Department of State. Current planning for extending telecommunications capabilities is based on a network capacity planning model that is constrained by funding and biased toward the past in assuming the preeminence of secure channels, the requirement for proprietary networks, and a modest expansion of current usage. The model does not anticipate the consolidation of USIA with the State Department, nor does it anticipate broadband multimedia connectivity among users.

Network planning also assumes three parallel networks to carry secure, sensitive, and Internet traffic respectively. Those entitled to access all three networks will require three desktop computers. Although some find this preposterous, it comes from a Cold War conviction that systems must be absolutely impenetrable. Although the incident may not even have occurred, a front page headline from *USA Today* highlights the problem that planners hope to avoid: "State Dept. suspects hacker—Computer system linking embassies was shut down."[138]

A preoccupation with absolute security has cut off diplomats from vital information. There is no question that systems must be secure, but they must also be functional. Instead of designing for zero risk, State should build systems that minimize risk to tolerable levels.

---

138. M. J. Zuckerman, "State Dept. suspects hacker—Computer system linking embassies was shut down," *USA Today*, March 23, 1998.

The department should oversee and install a single system, available on the desktop of each employee, with access to e-mail, the World Wide Web, and official traffic through sensitive and confidential. The system should make use of the Internet where it is available and proprietary channels where it is not. It should also be scalable so that it can be expanded by several magnitudes as usage requires. Cryptography should be used to protect sensitive and confidential materials.

> We haven't solved the problems that have been posed by the diplomatic security experts, haven't been able to build a sufficient firewall. We've got to solve that problem.
>
> —Richard M. Moose

Without minimizing the difficulty of solving the security problem, we are confident that it is a problem that can be solved satisfactorily by computer and security specialists.[139]

Computers

The State Department is currently replacing its proprietary Wang word processors after some 20 years of service. The new computers should all be in place by October 1999. The next phase of upgrading should begin immediately thereafter to avoid a repeat in two decades of the Wang predicament. Although support costs are significant, the cost of computers at $2,000 or less is a decreasing fraction of the necessary support required for the conduct of diplomacy.[140]

To stimulate usage and ensure future relevance, the Department should establish a capital fund for computer upgrading, allowing each user to upgrade or replace computers as needed. The Department of State, of course, would be responsible for maintaining the infrastructure and for specifying the type of equipment it would support. Individual users, then, could customize their computers as required for the performance of their work. Some, because of either the requirements of their position or their own work styles, would require infrequent upgrades. Heavy users, on the other hand, could be assured of state-of-the-art support. The management of this is not without its obvious problems, yet there is every reason, including efficiencies and value, to encourage the acquisition of tools to support the professional needs of diplomacy.

Foreign Affairs Network

The department should develop a fully integrated and comprehensive intranet to integrate information and processes. It would be accessed through a browser and linked through the telecommunications network described above. As the foreign affairs network developed, it would replace the current system of cable storage and retrieval. With the powerful search engines that are now available, there is little reason to continue key word tagging of cables. This network would become the corporate memory, the State Department's window on the world. The existing SIPRNET might serve as a model for this corporate intranet, even though State is not as active as other agencies in

---

139. Classified traffic at secret and above would continue to move through existing channels.

140. Infrastructure costs for each user—including cabling, switches, routers, and servers as well as software and support staff—are estimated by some industry analysts to be as high as $14,000 per year.

its use. Critics will find many reasons—including habit, cost, and security—why this network cannot be established, yet if State is to engage a broader community in its deliberations those objections must be overcome. Corporations have found solutions that provide protection of sensitive information.[141]

Computer literacy will inevitably be distributed along a normal curve with the most senior diplomats at the trailing edge. Consequently, the department should make the interface between user and computer excessively friendly. The computer desktop, with customized screens and drop-down menus, should be configured to provide easy access to the programs and Web sites in most frequent demand. As an integral part of the foreign affairs network, a customized foreign affairs desktop could be developed, updated annually at a token cost, and distributed on CD-ROMs to ensure that all users have common access to core materials.

> As long as we do not think of diplomacy as being in the communications business, we risk allowing it to continue in forms and procedures which were largely born of our last 50 years of experience and to be regarded in the future as quaint and largely irrelevant.
>
> —Charles A. Schmitz

Key Users

As computers grew up in accounting departments, they were seen primarily as tools for financial management and administration. The Wang word processors, on the other hand, have been used primarily as efficient typewriters by political and economic officers. The most progressive use of computers can be found at USIA and in Consular Affairs at the State Department, the latter because user fees could be applied to upgrading technology. Because of the different work cultures, policy officers should be given a greater say in the allocation of resources and the adoption of new software. Development of the foreign affairs network is a good place to start. Its core users would be located throughout the foreign affairs community. Ancillary users would include those outside of government who maintain their status in the reserve service. They, too, would have access through the level of confidential, with appropriate cryptography and security clearances.

Information Technology Resources

Although funding has been substantially increased for information technology, it may still be well below the new requirements. Views within the State Department are mixed. Our recommendations include both cost increases and savings but are not cost neutral. The panel recognizes that there are efficiencies to be gained by providing modern computers at a cost of less than $2,000 to diplomats whose salaries and benefits approach $100,000. Nonetheless, if the cost of appropriate information technology exceeds current appropriations, State should make a persuasive case to OMB and the Congress for another increase.

---

141. The foreign affairs network would not initially include materials classified above the level of confidential.

The most severe problem is largely hidden below the surface—recruitment, training, and retention of information management specialists. As long as the State Department remains a technological backwater and does not offer competitive salaries, it will be difficult to hire and retain the professionals required to manage modern systems in 250 locations. Attrition is far too high to build an information technology workforce to manage the systems of the future. State should adopt a dynamic model of future requirements including a mix of civil service, foreign service, foreign service nationals, and contractors to ensure quality service.

> The electric lightbulb made all kinds of things possible. It made it possible for people to read at night, but it didn't do the writing. The Internet makes information more readily available, but does not guarantee its accuracy.
>
> —Sanford J. Ungar

This section would not be complete without consideration of alternatives to manage the systems that have been described. The Department of Defense provides one alternative: the defense message system. Still under development, it holds promise of a secure, international network that can be used with a smart card coded with access information. The State Department should continue working with DOD to ensure that the system can be fully exploited.

Also, the State Department should consider outsourcing to commercial firms the management of one or more aspects of the telecommunications and computer systems described above. Citibank, for example, recently let a contract for its worldwide information management to an independent vendor. State may wish to consider this option, or at least demonstrate that it can provide comparable service at a comparable cost.

Finally, we recommend that State assign a knowledgeable planner to DARPA to ensure that the diplomatic community remains at the cutting edge of technology. Diplomacy cannot afford to fall further behind the information technology being developed by other elements of the federal government.

Move Public Diplomacy from the Sidelines to the Core of Diplomacy

DIPLOMACY MUST BE PROACTIVE IN PROMOTING U.S. POLICIES AND VALUES AND INTERACTIVE IN ENGAGING DOMESTIC AND FOREIGN PUBLICS.

Public Diplomacy Redefined

The consolidation of State and USIA affords an opportunity to redefine public diplomacy. USIA's mission statement is simple and clear: "to understand, inform, and influence foreign publics in promotion of the national interest and to broaden the dialogue between Americans and U.S. institutions and their counterparts abroad." Although the statement's clarity cannot be doubted, it must be reconsidered and restated to ensure that it fits comfortably in its new home at the Department of State. Furthermore, it must be given operational guidelines that will be respected at embassies around the world.

> In your report, you must start with some definition of public diplomacy. What role does it play today? How does it differ from the past?
>
> —Leonard H. Marks

The policy must reaffirm that propaganda, in the pejorative sense, is out—that education and information sharing are central. Although that is not a novel concept within USIA and Commerce, it runs counter to the State Department culture. A new balance must be found to reward transparency.

Smith-Mundt

The State Department and USIA have in the past year agreed on doctrinal distinctions between public diplomacy and public affairs—intended for foreign and domestic publics, respectively. These are distinctions that confuse instead of clarify. In a world with porous borders, messages can no longer be pigeonholed as domestic or foreign. What U.S. diplomats say in New Delhi is heard in New York.

Congress should repeal those portions of the 1948 Smith-Mundt Act that prohibit the domestic dissemination of programs designed for foreign publics and the 1985 Zorinsky amendment that prohibits USIA's use of appropriated funds to influence public opinion in the United States. We are confident that the legislation can be amended to avoid propaganda without placing on the State Department a restriction on public information that applies to no other element of the federal government.

NGO Relations

USAID has always had contractual relations with NGOs for services ranging from health care management to building civil societies. Likewise, USIA has given grants to NGOs to manage exchange programs. The State Department has, over the past two decades, given increased attention to NGOs as they have become an international political force. Nonetheless, the attention given is not commensurate with the evolving role of these organizations. Relations must go well beyond the occasional briefing or international conference. Diplomats should give as much attention to the major international NGOs as they do to Washington embassies. Routine personnel exchanges between State and the NGOs should be encouraged. A collaborative relationship should be fostered.

> I believe that the drift and direction of diplomacy will continue to be in the direction of more communication with publics and nongovernmental sectors of societies.
>
> —Joseph Duffey

Academic Relations

USIA and the State Department have enjoyed long-standing relations with the academic community, primarily through the Fulbright Program[142] and other academic exchange programs. Of the many exchange programs sponsored by the federal government, none is more important in sustaining America's international presence than the opportunity to study abroad. Globalization requires a cadre of workers in business, government, academe, and the NGO community who are well educated in the history, politics, and culture of other nations. However, the number of U.S. students studying

---

142. See *Fulbright at Fifty* (Research Triangle Park, N.C.: National Humanities Center, 1997), which concludes that the program's core mission of high-quality international exchange of students and scholars deserves greater support in the United States and abroad.

abroad, after remaining static for several decades, is now increasing only marginally. There are, for example, some 40,000 Japanese students studying in the United States compared with only a few thousand U.S. students studying in Japan, of whom only a handful are studying in the Japanese language.

We consequently recommend a government initiative to double the number of U.S. students studying abroad in the next decade. The programs that now support international education, including the Fulbright Student Program and the National Security Education Program, should be funded to ensure that this goal can be met.

It is further recommended that the State Department, with the consolidation of USIA, initiate a proactive relationship with the university community, expanding the diplomat-in-residence program, aggressively seeking academics for reserve appointments in the foreign service, and strengthening ongoing relations with the Association of Professional Schools of International Affairs. The aim should be to share experiences and encourage expansion of international education for the next generation of students.

Media Relations

The press is not the enemy. It is sometimes wrong, sometimes irresponsible, sometimes opinionated, sometimes irrelevant. But, most times, in democratic societies, it is an essential promoter and protector of freedom. Open diplomacy needs the press, and the press requires open diplomacy. Its recent neglect of international affairs is to be deplored, yet the press cannot be blamed when national leaders are preoccupied with other matters and the schools ignore the rest of the world. There is an urgency to engage leaders, publics, and the press in the great international issues of our time. It is the continuing role of diplomacy to inform and educate, to be proactive as well as reactive, to step out of the shadow of anonymity and engage the public in a spirited discussion. This description sounds like the best practices of USIA abroad and State's public affairs unit. It is also among the best practices of some of the nation's most effective ambassadors. The next step is to broaden the number of interlocutors so that every ambassador is a public ambassador and every diplomat a public diplomat.

> Because we are a great power, we should act like a great power, we should be willing to put resources into public diplomacy and take it seriously because the whole world is, in fact, our stage.
>
> —David R. Gergen

Broadcasting

VOA, RFE, and the other broadcasting services constitute the largest single program within USIA's budget. In the current consolidation plan, the broadcast services are to become an independent government organization under the direction of the BBG. To manage the transition from shortwave to the new digital technologies, the BBG should establish a broadcast technology planning unit. Staffed with engineers and visionaries, it should be charged with imagining the future and advising the BBG.

As a first step, the BBG should inaugurate a global affairs channel on the Internet with real-time audio and video streaming.[143] The service would be established as a global forum for government, NGOs, and academic communities to strengthen cooperation and address urgent global issues. In content, it would serve as an international analog to the domestic C-Span in the United States. In style, it would be reflective of the new information era: interactive, inclusive, engaging. Although Internet access is severely limited today in many countries, within a decade it will be available practically everywhere. The price of admission is no longer measured in kilowattage or broadcast hours but in the quality and presentation of the information.

> Embrace the new technology. Don't be repelled by it. It is not there to hurt you. It is there to help you. That's a really important part of the new diplomacy.
>
> —Marvin Kalb

The BBG should also establish additional surge capacity for crisis broadcasting to support U.S. diplomatic initiatives. Such broadcasts might be short-lived during a crisis or sustained for years when totalitarian regimes restrict the free flow of information. It is time for the United States to consider its responsibility when rogue regimes use the media as a weapon of death, as witnessed in Bosnia and Rwanda. Inciting citizens to murder their ethnic or political rivals is not some kind of global First Amendment activity. Should the BBG aggressively act to counter these hate broadcasts? Should the U.S. Army set up field radios as part of its psychological operations? These are questions to which the technical answers are easy and the policy answers complex—but they are not questions that can be ignored.

In addition to a VOA Web site, the State Department will continue to require an official presence it can call its own. We consequently recommend consolidation of the USIA and State presence on the World Wide Web under the direction of a staff that is policy sensitive, technically competent, and enormously creative. If there are a million sites to chose from today, there will be 10 million tomorrow. State's site not only must be the site of record on a vast range of international issues but must be sophisticated enough to attract interested American and foreign publics.

Focus Greater Attention and Place a Higher Priority on Commercial Diplomacy

To ensure u.s. competitiveness in the global economy, the united states must strengthen its ability to expand global markets and assist u.s. business abroad.

The government's role as mediator, moderator, and facilitator is critical because of the accelerating consequences of national policies. Diplomacy, as manifest through several departments and agencies, has a major advocacy role in insisting on a level playing field for U.S. business. To a lesser extent, diplomacy also has an advisory and promotional role in the developing world. Government is not, however, a surrogate for the U.S. business and

> I believe the business community needs to play a very different role and needs to be garnered as a partner, as a voice, as a support group for the foreign service.
>
> —Lauri J. Fitz-Pegado

---

143. See <www.voa.gov> for examples of RealAudio offered by VOA. With appropriate software, both video and audio streaming can be accessed on <www.broadcast.com>. Examples from Harvard and Yale are available at <www.ksg.harvard.edu> and <info.med.yale.edu/EIINet>.

financial community abroad. Although government must perform with excellence, it cannot pretend to assume roles that belong to the private sector. The recommendations that follow reflect the progress made by Commerce, USTR, and others in recognizing the changing needs of the U.S. business community.

Commercial Officers

If thinking globally but acting locally is the key to success in global business, the service provided to business on the ground must be the locus of reform. The Department of Commerce is represented abroad in 70 locations, the Department of Agriculture in 80 locations; both are staffed by career foreign service officers. In smaller embassies, State's economic officers serve also as commercial officers. It is fair to say that the function does not enjoy the same status as economic or political reporting, yet its return can be significant. It is essential that the status of commercial officers be enhanced, commensurate with their role abroad.

> I don't think we have been as assiduous in rearranging, if you like, the pecking order in our embassies in the direction of economics, as have some of our competitor nations, like Germany.
>
> —Joseph LaPalombara

The new diplomacy requires more commercial officers, better attuned to the needs of U.S. business. The most effective officers, whether from Commerce, State, or Agriculture, are those who are well briefed about leading sectors of business and technology, sectors where the United States excels and wishes to expand markets. Training, which tends to focus on process, must be expanded to include telecommunications, transport, banking, and financial services.

In addition to high standards in the recruiting and training of commercial officers, the panel recommends a comprehensive one-for-one exchange with the U.S. business community. Career commercial officers should spend at least one assignment with a U.S. corporation as a requirement for promotion to the senior ranks of the foreign service. In turn, corporations should be persuaded to exchange officials to serve an overseas tour as part of the reserve service. Great Britain has already pioneered such an exchange. The United States should not be far behind. To be more than a token nod, the exchange would require a substantial long-term commitment by government and business. Because the record on exchanges between government and business is uneven, both parties would have to ensure that only their most promising employees were offered in exchange.

Responsibilities expected of exchanged officers must be clearly delineated. Both the government and the corporation need to be precise about the experiences their employees will have. A foreign service officer on detail should have a mix of corporate headquarters and field experience and should be given access to corporate finance, planning, sales, and product development. Most of all, the officer on detail needs hands-on business experience, working in tandem with a business professional.

Ambassador as Advocate

Because the U.S. ambassador plays the key role in steering the mission's commercial activities, the ambassador must be well prepared through experience or training to advocate fair access to U.S. business. Particularly when an ambassador is assigned to an emerging market, one of the most important functions is to use the ambassadorial authority and wit to convince national and local authorities to revise policies, laws,

and regulations that restrict U.S. business. As many U.S. ambassadors already give considerable time to commercial advocacy, the panel urges that the function be more widely recognized and better supported.

> The United States government has to be prepared to spend more time, effort, and energy in supporting American business abroad, American investment abroad, and so forth.
>
> —Lawrence S. Eagleburger

Commercial diplomacy, moreover, must not stop at capitals. To assist U.S. business, diplomats must follow the markets by moving out of capitals into cities and regions where business is booming. The practice initiated by Ambassador Felix Rohatyn—reassigning officers from Paris to regional business centers—should be the model of the future if diplomacy is to strengthen its service to U.S. business.[144] What cannot be done in Paris can often be accomplished in Lyon or Lille.

U.S. Business and Information Centers

Exceptional opportunities exist for U.S. business and finance in what the Commerce Department calls the big emerging markets (BEMs)—including China, India, and Mexico. Here, too, is the greatest opportunity for diplomacy to assist business in navigating through cultural and political barriers. The advisory panel recommends the creation of a public–private consortium, supported by public and private funds, to develop and manage U.S. business and information centers in these 10 BEMs. The centers, designed to generate new opportunities for investment and trade, would serve as physical and electronic meeting places for U.S. and host-country business representatives. Parties to the funding and management would include, but not be limited to, the Department of State, Department of Commerce, Department of Agriculture, U.S. corporations, and U.S. higher education. Physically modest, they would serve as centers of electronic connectivity with high-bandwidth digital access to U.S. corporations and government. The centers would be staffed by foreign service career and reserve officers, including seconded corporate executives. With a long-term investment by business and government, they would be more ambitious than the several cooperative models that the Commerce Department opened in Jakarta, Shanghai, and Sao Paulo and more comprehensive than the business information centers in Europe.

Global Center for Commerce and Finance

Where does a representative of a U.S. corporation doing business abroad turn for help in Washington? The correct answer is the Department of Commerce; but it is also the Department of Agriculture, the Department of Energy, the Department of Transportation, the Department of Justice, the Department of the Treasury, and the Department of State. The alphabet soup of ExIm, OPIC, and TDA[145] is not the easiest to navigate for those outside of Washington. To encourage small business to develop

---

144. Jim Hoagland, "Ambassador of Business," *Washington Post*, June 19, 1998.

145. Export–Import Bank of the United States, Overseas Private Investment Corporation, and Trade and Development Agency

international markets, the government must find a way to simplify access to its many resources. The Department of Commerce should establish a global center for commerce and finance, a one-stop information shopping center. As well as a physical space in Washington, it should have a user-friendly presence on the World Wide Web that can be accessed by U.S. business from any location.

Global Negotiations

Commercial diplomacy requires multinational and binational negotiations for reducing trade barriers, developing enforcement regimes, aggressive monitoring of treaties, and leveling the international trading field through the use of the global bully pulpit. Particular attention must be given to intellectual property rights, telecommunications deregulation, and trade in services. The Office of the U.S. Trade Representative, with a staff of well under 200 employees, is forced to rely on short-term, largely untrained detailees. It is swamped by numerous demands, both substantive and political, and needs more resources for negotiating and monitoring compliance. The opportunities are staggering. The return on investment can be enormous.

> Coordination among governments on macroeconomic policies, efforts among governments to deal with nontariff barriers or intellectual property rights—all the issues that are raised more by globalization become more important.
>
> —Anthony Lake

Multilateral Diplomacy

The World Bank, the IMF, and the WTO (successor to the General Agreement on Tariffs and Trade [GATT]) are the three pillars of the postwar economic regime. They have had unprecedented success in lowering tariff barriers, increasing world trade, and stimulating international development. Notwithstanding their successes, the changing international economic environment dictates that they not cling to past practices. Decisions once made behind closed doors must be open to public scrutiny. Transparency and accountability are essential. Pending necessary reforms, however, the United States cannot afford to neglect, withhold funds from, or otherwise marginalize these institutions. For example, the United States can enhance the WTO's new regulatory agreements by contributing expertise on telecommunications deregulation, which will eventually open up additional opportunities for U.S. business. In short, the panel recommends the continuation of strong U.S. leadership, staffing, and support for these international organizations.

Another opportunity for multilateral diplomacy is the promotion of international acceptance of the standards governing U.S. corporations as provided in the Foreign Corrupt Practices Act (FCPA). Because our foreign competitors are not similarly constrained, U.S. business frequently loses its competitive advantage. Diplomatic efforts undertaken by the United States to multilateralize the FCPA in the OECD need to be given more attention. Moreover, it is important for U.S. embassies to act aggressively when corruption undercuts the competitiveness of U.S. companies and undermines the vitality of national economies.

For All of This to Happen...

THE DEPARTMENT OF STATE, WITH THE SUPPORT OF THE NSC, SHOULD DEVELOP A PLAN OF ACTION TO REFORM THE CULTURE OF DIPLOMACY AND UPGRADE THE QUALITY OF TECHNOLOGY. NEITHER RENEWAL NOR REFORM WILL OCCUR WITHOUT EXTRA-ORDINARY DIRECTION AND LEADERSHIP.

Both diplomatic culture and technology must change. Each will, in turn, change the other in a virtuous cycle of reform and renewal. There is no quick fix, however, for the antici-pated scale of change. James Champy, coauthor of *Reengineering the Corporation*, says, "...it takes at least five years of persistent effort and outstanding leadership to make cultural change work."[146]

> We need a vision for a new public-state diplomacy, we called it New Diplomacy in our commission report. That's a real vision. That's a vision that you can sell to the American people.
>
> —Lewis Manilow

The State Department should know. What has come, for example, of the Strategic Management Initiative launched several years ago? Or of the Thomas Report, the Bremer Report, the Veliotes Report, or State 2000? Renewal, reform, and reinvention require an ambitious action plan. Good intentions must be translated into bold deeds:

Change Leadership

The first and most important step is to designate a change leader. Some, insisting that the Defense Department would not have changed without several secretaries who played that role, argue that it must be the secretary of state. Others say, "No, the secre-tary cannot give the necessary time; it must be the deputy secretary." Some have suggested recruiting a distinguished change leader from the private sector, yet that per-son would be handicapped by having neither the authority nor the institutional knowledge to lead profound change. Still oth-ers have suggested the task be given to an under secretary or a distinguished career diplo-mat, either of whom would enjoy the complete confidence of the secretary of state.

> We're engaged in a new reorganization effort here in the State Department to find ways to be better stewards of the public resources because in the last analysis, the major focus of all of our reorganization efforts has to be a more efficient State Department.
>
> —Thomas Pickering

In fact, it matters too much to delegate the leadership role. Only the secretary of state can lead this process—and only with support from the administration, the Congress, the career service, and the U.S. public. The secretary should designate a senior executive team from State, USAID, USIA, Commerce, Agriculture, and other agencies that deal in foreign affairs to oversee the management of change.

Fortune magazine recently surveyed executives, directors, and security analysts to identify America's most admired companies. At the top of the list were General Elec-tric, Microsoft, Coca-Cola, Intel, and Hewlett-Packard, followed by Southwest Airlines, Berkshire Hathaway, Disney, Johnson & Johnson, and Merck. The single ele-ment that distinguished them from the rest of the pack was leadership. "The truth is

---

146. James Champy, "Loony-tunes management training," *Forbes* (November 17, 1997): 156.

that no one factor makes a company admirable, but if you were forced to pick the one that makes the most difference, you'd pick leadership."[147]

Management Advisory Council

The Department of State is not the only player in the conduct of diplomacy, even if it is the core institution. To expand the reach of the change effort, a management advisory council of seven to nine distinguished leaders should be named by the vice president through the National Partnership for Reinventing Government. Representatives would be selected from corporations, NGOs, universities, the media, the military, and government. They would meet periodically for one year to advise the secretary on the management of change.

Compact with Congress

Congressional support of change in the culture and technology of diplomacy is imperative. The Department of Defense could not have undertaken its revolution in military affairs without congressional support. Neither can State fundamentally change diplomacy without the active support of Congress. Legislation such as Smith-Mundt will have to be amended. Consolidation will have to be completed. Resources will have to be increased. The president should propose a compact with Congress to share in leading the reinvention of diplomacy.

Ambassadors

Washington must lead the change agenda. Ambassadors must execute it overseas. It is time for the announcement and application of new standards for the appointment of political and career ambassadors to signal both a renewal of professionalism and a redelegation of authority to embassies. The release of former president Richard Nixon's taped conversations revealing a price on ambassadorships should be sufficient to terminate the practice; but in the event it is not, we urge AFSA, the American Academy of Diplomacy, and the Council of American Ambassadors to collaborate in publicly assessing candidates as an aid to the executive branch and the Senate in their consideration of the competence of future nominees—including both political and career appointees.

> It is crucial that an ambassador be able to get on television in a foreign country, speak the language, and explain the policy of the United States.
>
> —Marvin Kalb

If ambassadors are to lead successfully the new diplomacy, they must be expert at communicating with publics and representing U.S. commercial interests as well as possess the traditional skills of diplomacy. Except for the rare individual, professional training for these new roles will be required. The brief orientation now offered to new U.S. ambassadors by the Department of State must be significantly enhanced.

---

147. Thomas A. Stewart, "Why Leadership Matters," *Fortune* (March 2, 1998): 72.

Timelines, Benchmarks, and Best Practices

Without a timeline for change, the best of plans fades away. The plan should have ambitious and detailed change goals for the first year, changes so bold they cannot be ignored. The timeline should extend five years into the future and be subject to continual modification as actions are completed, accelerated, or delayed. The planners should be inspired by optimism yet guided by practicality. Benchmarking comparable practices from industry or other elements of government should be an integral part of the change plan. Routinely practiced in progressive corporations, benchmarking is used to ensure competitiveness by introducing efficiencies, reducing overhead, and improving quality. Corporations are also collecting and sharing best practices, tools and techniques developed in one office or location that others can use. The exchange of information not only introduces change but supports the collaborative model that this study encourages.

Resources

Diplomacy cannot return to a state of readiness as long as its operating budget continues to be cut. The ambitious changes that are recommended herein cannot be undertaken without additional resources for technology, training, and communications. As this study is concluding, an administration request for a supplemental appropriation to upgrade embassy security enjoys bipartisan congressional support. That decision should be followed by swift action by OMB and Congress to provide the necessary additional resources for reinventing the conduct of diplomacy.

Conclusion

This study has focused on the conduct of diplomacy in the Information Age. A larger and related issue is the development and management of foreign policy. As a postscript, the advisory panel believes that the National Security Act of 1947 should be revisited. The foreign policy machinery, including the role of the NSC staff and the process of decisionmaking, warrants a thorough examination.[148] Indeed, as the strategies of the current study are adopted, the shape of future structural change will undoubtedly become more evident.

> What we have been observing in this century, particularly the last part of this century, is probably greater in its significance than any act since the discovery of fire by primitive man.
>
> —Max M. Kampelman

At the century's end, U.S. leadership is unrivaled. U.S. business is booming. U.S. higher education is unsurpassed. U.S. technology is transforming the world. And what of U.S. diplomacy? To sustain dynamic stability in a complex world, it must be guided by coherence, capability, discipline, and agility. It must be characterized by openness and permeability. It must change now.

---

148. Cambone, *A New Structure for National Security Policy Planning.*

APPENDIX I

Interview Analysis

Interviews by Barry Fulton, project director, with 68 experts were conducted, recorded, and summarized during the period July 11, 1997–October 8, 1997. Respondents, who are listed at the end of this appendix, are identified with the positions they held at the time of the interviews; they included 57 members of the advisory panel plus 11 other officials, diplomats, and scholars. Complete transcriptions of the interviews are available on the CSIS Web site <www.csis.org> at the section on International Communications Studies.

The findings, organized by the six identical questions used in each of the interviews, cover several major topics: global civil society, redefining U.S. diplomacy, embassy priorities, media and information technology, communicating with foreign publics, and brave new digital world.

Global Civil Society

QUESTION: As we celebrate the 50th anniversary of the Marshall Plan, we seem to be hesitant to continue our active international engagement. Although there is little reluctance to fund activities that directly enhance American security and prosperity, according to a poll by the Chicago Council on Foreign Relations, the American public no longer supports government expenditures directed at (a) defending human rights in other countries, (b) helping bring about democratic governments, (c) protecting weaker nations against foreign aggression, or (d) improving the standard of living of less developed nations. Some argue, on the other hand, that we should actively promote such causes abroad. Let's start with this question: Is it in our national interest to do so, that is to tax American citizens to help strengthen what I would call global civil society?

Apple Pie, Motherhood, and Civil Society

"Yes, unequivocally, absolutely, certainly, clearly, obviously!" With these and similar expressions, most of the respondents agreed that fostering global civil society is in the U.S. national interest:

> It is an old-fashioned notion and one easily denigrated by references to everything from the Munich syndrome to the hangover of a Cold War mentality, but it seems clear to me that our enduring security depends on an international environment which is as safe as possible for the kinds of values that we cherish. (Carter)

However, there emerged a fair number of distinctions of means, costs, and public perceptions.

79

Equivocation

Even as many agreed with the desirability of promoting global civil society, there were numerous expressions of doubt about our ability to play this role through traditional means:

> Historically we've been very clumsy in doing that, and we've done a lot more harm than good. (Anable) ⌣ In the past much of this has been wasted money. (Sheridan) ⌣ If we know the policies that would produce an improvement in civil society and if we had the capacity to carry those policies out, it would be in the national interest. (Hedblom) ⌣ People have become persuaded that most of these efforts are fruitless. (Grossman) ⌣ I hope we are learning that they are naive in many cases and counterproductive. (Lange)

Resources

Reflecting the ambiguity of the question, respondents represented a broad range of opinions:

> The connection between spending these monies and the desired outcomes is unclear, and I personally would argue that it is not a good way to spend taxpayers' dollars. (Bray)

Others leaned in the opposite direction:

> To my mind, the need to promote civil society and to use taxpayers dollars to do so is more compelling than ever. (Frost)

While intellectual and political differences should not be bridged by searching for neutral language, the sense of disquiet in the responses between means and ends suggests that a sense of proportion is missing:

> We have to have regard to an appropriate proportion between the cost of these things and the real prospect of achieving tangible results. (Moose)

In seeking the right proportion, some suggest, we should examine the entire national security budget:

> With respect to international affairs the issue is not, I suspect, shall we spend more money for diplomatic priorities, but shall we spend less on traditional defense in order to spend more on new diplomatic priorities? (Duffey) ⌣ The ratio is $250 billion for defense, $30 billion for intelligence, and about $19 billion for everything else; this nation has it dramatically wrong in terms of the ratios and in terms of the effectiveness. (Harris)

Several pointed out the striking differences between expenditures on foreign assistance and the public perception:

> Recent polling data has indicated that most Americans are favorable to foreign assistance but believe almost violently that we overspend. When asked what the ideal figure would be, they cite 5 percent, which as you know is 5 times what we

currently spend. (Pickering) ∼ The perception that resources spent overseas are resources taken away from what could be spent in ameliorating social conditions here will continue to be a concern. (Quainton) ∼ The problem has been that they think they are spending a lot more and getting a lot less. (Nelson)

Public Opinion

Many respondents commented on the Chicago Council poll results—agreeing, disagreeing, clarifying, and reinterpreting:

> There's no question that the most recent Chicago Council on Foreign Relations national public opinion study showed that when it came to what you call global civil society issues, or humanitarian issues, there has been a substantial shift in attitudes since the end of the Cold War. (Rielly) ∼ It's undoubtedly true that the public as a whole has much less interest in what's happening abroad today. (Cutler)

Others suggested that there has been no real change:

> The public in general—I'm not sure that they have ever of their own volition supported such activities. (Burnett) ∼ I'm not sure that for most of the last 40 or 50 years, the question put to them in a generic sense would ever get much support. (Eagleburger)

Still others suggested that the support is there, but the questions were too abstract to tap people's feelings:

> The polls are misleading, at least in a practical sense, in that when that question is asked in the abstract, people will say "no". (Lake) ∼ The American public is relatively impatient with abstract discussions of foreign policy, but tend to react much more affirmatively once it's presented with a concrete case and a strong argument. (Mora)

And others suggested the poll was wrong:

> …interesting but probably not very accurate. (Reid) ∼ I do not agree with the Chicago findings. (Marks)

Although there is no consensus on the issue, there appears to be broad support for engaging publics on international issues:

> It's not possible to have any sustained peacetime foreign policy initiative without public support. (Robison)

Leadership

If there was no agreement on public opinion, there was a resounding consensus on the failure of U.S. leadership:

> What that poll for me reflects is not necessarily a problem with the American society as much as a problem with the leadership of our society. (Kampelman) ∼

There is a vacuum; without clear leadership from the bully pulpit of the presidency, I do not see how we can reinvigorate the public interest and the public understanding of our stake in a United States that is activist internationally. (Bloch) ∼ The problem is that the Congress, the congressional leadership is really very unknowledgable about the world, and we have not had sufficient public articulators of the role that the United States must play. (Harris) ∼ The government and all of us in the foreign policy racket need to do much more to show American citizens how almost everything that we are doing abroad is somehow related to their everyday lives. (Lake) ∼ You could alter that public mood considerably by public leadership at the top levels of American political life. (Carter) ∼ This is uniquely an area that requires American leadership. (Cowan)

A senior State Department official spoke of Secretary of State Albright's recognition of the importance of leadership:

Leadership in these questions is something that she's already had a lot of experience in, and I think it is having a significant effect on the national view of these particular issues. (Pickering)

End of the Cold War

Many described the end of the Cold War as a defining moment in the conduct of international relations:

Engagement is changing dramatically with the end of the Cold War. (Solomon) ∼ There is no longer a clear enemy. (Bloch) ∼ We don't have anyone foreign to unite against at the moment. (Cutler) ∼ Once the threat of the Cold War is gone, the unifying theme of American foreign policy for the last 50 years or so has disappeared. (McHenry) ∼ Now people are saying it's over, let's go back to our more normal state. (Zorthian) ∼ The problem is that we have a national history that has a very strong residue of noninvolvement, unless it is in terms of having to deal with some really very easily identifiable demon out there. (LaPalombara) ∼ The end of the Cold War has produced a retrenchment, not only of America's judgment as to where it ought to apply its resources but of America's vision of its own responsibilities to the rest of the world. (Kalb)

Search for a New Vision

Some called for a vision that publics can understand and spoke of the

…failure of elites, especially in Washington, to articulate a vision of a future world and what America's interests in that world are. (Gergen) ∼ There is confusion about the broad goals and about the means to achieve them. (Kornblum)

Although the public cannot be expected to rally around abstractions, it will understand an appeal to not only self-interest but also the country's basic values:

We are, for better or for worse, children of a notion of our own exceptionalism; a part of that is myth, but I think that it is attempting to live up to myths that keep a nation strong and vital and clean in its own terms. (Carter) ∽ America, in the eyes of the world, stands for a set of values. (Moose) ∽ The United States is, unlike virtually any other society, one that's created on the basis of an idea. (Fukuyama) ∽ Part of the reason why Americans are asked by their government to support human rights promotion is American self-respect. (Henrikson) ∽ Americans understand that we do have not only an opportunity but the privilege of being able to help strengthen global civil society while not having to sacrifice anything at home, and that to strengthen civil society elsewhere, strengthens us. (Ungar)

Although there are hints of a vision that might generate public support, neither clarity nor consensus emerged from the interviews.

The British Example

In contrast, interviews with two British scholars and a British strategist suggest a more coherent national vision in Great Britain. One spoke of a

…high moral focus that it is our responsibility as global citizens to help the disadvantaged, to ameliorate abuses of human rights of all kinds, and that the appropriate aim of our national policy ought to be to reorientate our efforts and our expenditures in foreign policy to that end. (Hemery)

Another suggested that developing consensus is easier there than in the United States because

…in Britain, there is a more homogeneous society, a more dense geographical setting, and more sense of the immediacy of the external environment. (Hocking) ∽ There is a cross-party consensus in the United Kingdom that seems to be accepted by most of the people of Britain—that the privilege which we enjoy as a permanent member of the UN Security Council brings with it obligations as well, that the history which we all in Britain have inherited, that is, the history of having been a major colonial power at one time, a world superpower, also brings with it obligations. (Newton)

Communications

Even with a coherent vision and willing leadership, the public will not rally to support international engagement without effective communications:

There is a major communication gap between the traditional foreign policy establishment and the American public. (Burt) ∽ There has to be some kind of sustained public education, not undertaken necessarily by the government, but by some coalition of groups and individuals for whom that is an agenda. (Robison)

Several have observed that when the public understands the stakes, it will rally behind U.S. leadership. One respondent wrote of public responses to the Iran–Iraq war:

Eventually you would find, even in a sort of distant, obscure, unfathomable, ungraspable situation like that, people would say, "Isn't this ridiculous; can't we do something? We're so smart. We're so sensible. Can't we do something to help these people stop killing each other's children?" (Ungar)

Redefining U.S. Diplomacy

QUESTION: The State Department says "the purpose of United States foreign policy is to create a more secure, prosperous, and democratic world for the benefit of the American people."[1] Great Britain's former foreign secretary Douglas Hurd spoke in 1996 of three functions of diplomacy: (a) the accumulation and analysis of information, (b) negotiation, and (c) the promotion of national interests—including "trade, finance, politics, culture, and tourism."[2] Others have argued that the most important functions of modern diplomacy are (d) preventive diplomacy and crisis management, (e) facilitation of commerce, (f) promoting human rights, and (g) safeguarding the global environment. In addition, diplomats are responsible for (h) assisting American citizens abroad, (i) providing humanitarian assistance, and now (j) battling terrorism, drugs, and weapons proliferation. If you were defining—or redefining—American diplomacy for the twenty-first century, what would be your priorities?

Complexity

The most frequent response to the question was "all of the above":

> There's no reason why all the ideas which the question put forward should not be high on a foreign policy agenda. (Newton)

There was also a recognition that the suggested goals and functions of diplomacy are not necessarily in harmony:

> When you get down to specific issues, those goals oftentimes are in conflict. (Burt)

State's comprehensive response to managing this complexity has resulted in what one respondent called "an action plan for God." (Harris)

The world in which modern diplomacy is conducted, many suggested, is a fundamentally different place:

> What we've been observing in this century, particularly the last part of this century, is probably greater in its significance than any act since the discovery of fire by primitive man. (Kampelman)

Respondents spoke of a world that is totally interdependent, interconnected, interrelated, and economically integrated:

> One of the highest priorities is simply being able to cope with the multiplicity of demands simultaneously. (Schwartz)

---

1. Department of State, *United States Strategic Plan for International Affairs* (September 1997) <http://www.state.gov/www/global/general_foreign_policy/spia_index.html>.
2. Douglas Hurd, "Has Diplomacy a Future?" (Ditchley Foundation Lecture XXXIII, Oxfordshire County, United Kingdom, 1996).

To cope, respondents suggested approaches they described as contextual, holistic, and seat-of-the-pants.

Globalization

The "globalization of almost everything" (Carter) was a recurring theme of the interviews. Although economic globalization was routinely cited, several suggested that the phenomenon extends well beyond trade and economic issues to security, environment, and human values:

> Our national interests are rarely that distinct from the common good of a much larger community. (Burnett)

The global community that is emerging may require a diplomacy different from that bounded by the rise of the nation-state and the half century of the Cold War:

> Traditional diplomacy doesn't seem to take into account that globalization is a fact of life on many, many levels, many of which are not susceptible to quantification or measurement. (Robison)

Globalization, however defined, has been accelerated by rapid development in communications:

> It's getting closer to one world in the '90s, with communications technology which permits people to know what's going on everywhere. (Manilow)

In summary, the world of diplomacy is undergoing an unprecedented change:

> There is no question that globalization has changed the relationships among states, the ways in which the world affects the citizens of every state, and the relative power of governments to act effectively, both internationally and within their own societies. (Lake)

Leadership

The need for U.S. leadership—domestically and internationally—was repeatedly cited:

> People expect leadership from us around the world; there is no other leader of global stature comparable to the United States. (Frost)

Some assume that U.S. leadership is a given:

> America has, at this stage, more capacity for leadership than perhaps at any time in the past, including the very seminal period following the end of the Second World War. (Pickering)

On the other hand, some believe that the government has been too reactive in the post–Cold War period:

> I have been struck in my work at the State Department at how frequently we were responding rather than leading—responding because we can't predict or control or prevent the conflicts from arising. (Schneider)

Ends and Means

Many respondents distinguished between the broad goals of diplomacy and the means by which it is conducted:

> American diplomacy is first and foremost a means to an end; the real question is what are the ends. (Gergen)

Although agreement on goals is paramount, several emphasized the necessity of attending to the tools and processes of diplomacy, the art of observation, analysis, negotiation, and representation:

> When you are building up your diplomacy, you should build up those structures and the cadre of people whose job it is to maximize the use of all kinds of resources to achieve whatever goals are set for them by the political leadership or by the country. (Kornblum)

National Security

A great many agreed that the foremost goal of diplomacy is protecting the security of the state:

> What really has to be at the top of our list is the security of the United States, whatever the hell that means. (Eagleburger)

What that meant to respondents includes a range of regional and country-specific concerns (Europe, Middle East, China, Russia, Japan, Turkey, Iraq), traditional concerns (proliferation, terrorism), and newer transnational issues (environment, drugs, information warfare, international crime, disease). Some emphasized the need for crisis prevention and crisis management:

> That is one of the most difficult things to explain to the American people, because if you prevent something from happening, it's not really easy to make it clear what you accomplished. (Eagleburger)

In summary, the primary purpose of diplomacy, most agree, is

> …the perpetuation of an international environment which is not hostile to or dangerous to the United States. (Carter) ∼ Making sure that we are secure is obviously goal number one. (Johnstone)

Economic Prosperity

A sizable number put economic prosperity at the top of their lists:

> Obviously, economic interests are number one. (de Borchgrave)

Respondents spoke of the need for broad international activities—promoting open markets, reducing nontariff barriers, supporting intellectual property rights—as well as country-specific trade promotion:

> The highest priority of our diplomacy should be to assure the competitiveness of the United States as an economic unit in the world economy. (LaPalombara)

The argument that supporting economic development builds world stability was also advanced:

> My priorities would lie in the economic and commercial arena because I believe that's the backbone of building stable countries, democratic nations, nations that are able to feed themselves, that are able to have their infrastructures grow, that are able to walk into the twenty-first century with new technologies. (Fitz-Pegado)

A Missing Goal?

Whereas a significant number agreed that protecting U.S. security and promoting prosperity were fundamental goals of diplomacy, promoting democracy did not emerge as a coequal goal. Only a few placed it high among their priorities:

> My first priority would be promoting democracy. (Fouhy)

Others asserted primacy for human rights:

> I definitely would put questions of human rights ahead of the simple question of democracy. (Burnett)

But there were dissenters as well:

> There is a streak of hypocrisy in the United States judging every country in terms of moral human rights consideration. (Fromm)

Several spoke of other related concerns: representation of U.S. culture, the promotion of civil society, and the advancement of U.S. values.

Although respondents gave a collective sense of leaning toward a common vision, it remained inchoate:

> What is a problem is when we don't set these objectives in a larger context of vision, if you like—a portrait of a civil society that works as an ideal to be achieved. (Frost)

There is a sense that something is missing:

> It's too bad because none of those reflect the flavor of what has got to be a foundation beneath security, trade, and human rights. It's got to be a very different approach to dialogue and exchange and information dealing with what is really on most people's minds, which is not foreign policy in the first place, or even foreign economic policy, and certainly not human rights. (Hitchcock)

There is the hint of a broader and underlying goal of diplomacy among several of the respondents:

> The framework for the State Department should be relationship building for the long term. (Etheredge)

Although the distinction between means and ends reemerges, it seems clear that the study must accommodate the feeling that security and prosperity are insufficient goals of diplomacy. Perhaps the third element is what Joseph Nye called "soft power" or Kenneth Boulding labeled "integrative power" in contrast with "threat power" and "economic power": "The stick, the carrot, and the hug may all be necessary, but the greatest of these is the hug."[3]

Environmental and Population Issues

The global environment is one of the issues that provoked considerable comment:

> The twenty-first century is going to be the century of the environment, replacing the century of potential nuclear holocaust. (Anable)

Improving the environment is so complex that it "almost has to be a national and international public responsibility across national lines." (Henrikson)

Population growth and the attendant poverty were also cited as concerns warranting our attention:

> That is an issue that could explode in our faces at any time. (Gergen) ∼ [W]e have 90 million new babies every year in the world, most of them born into the megaslums of the Third World, [which are] the ingredients for major trouble in the years ahead. (de Borchgrave)

On the other hand, some suggested that environmental concerns are politically correct, are critical, but are outside of the reach of diplomacy, and look important because the world is at peace.

Embassy Priorities

QUESTION: Assume you have just been named as ambassador to a country where we are seeking to strengthen relations. Your budget for conducting diplomacy is fixed, but within that budget you can use your resources any way you choose. The embassy has a staff of 70 Americans, including political officers, economic officers, consular officers, public affairs officers, defense attachés, commercial officers, agricultural attachés, intelligence officers, representatives from several other federal agencies, as well as specialists in administration, communications, and security. What functions would you strengthen? Which ones might you reduce or eliminate?

Customizing Embassies

There was broad agreement that functions and staffing have "to be customized, tailored to the situation of a particular country." (Zorthian)

> By gosh, the world is a strange and different place, and almost every country is different, so that to look at a country model for the judgment of resources would

---

3. Kenneth Boulding, *The Three Faces of Power* (Newbury Park, Calif.: Sage, 1989), 250.

lead to distortions. (Pickering) ∼ Surely, if I go as ambassador to London, I have different priorities than if I go as ambassador to Uzbekistan. (Roberts) ∼ Obviously Haiti is going to be different from Russia. (Powell)

Suggestions ranged from strengthening consular functions to outsourcing administrative functions, from improving open source reporting to reducing intelligence functions:

You have to analyze each country according to its characteristics and determine what the mix should be. (Marks)

Several argued for greater flexibility in structuring and staffing embassies:

Our current embassies are structured to mirror personnel systems that were created in another time and for another purpose. (Quainton)

A few suggested reducing the size of our Embassies:

Most of the embassies are overbloated and should be slimmed down. (Hauser) ∼ My first recommendation would be to reduce the staff. (de Borchgrave)

Authority and Style

Despite a long-standing presidential directive, one respondent observed that

…the ambassador has to balance without power—power that can be checked by cabinet heads, or whatever, or even other parts of the State Department. (Cutler) ∼ The buck should stop at the ambassador's desk in terms of everything that's happening, including monitoring what other agencies of the American government are doing. (Etheredge)

Several spoke of the need to integrate skillfully the functions in our embassies:

The greatest concern I would have is simply to make the parts work together. (Harrington) ∼ We must tailor our programs, the usage of our staff within missions, the definition of the mission statement, the coordination among agencies of the U.S. government, and the nature of what the ambassador is. (Fitz-Pegado)

A few commented on problems among the law enforcement agencies, including their recent growth:

I still do not believe they have fully accepted the discipline of the country team. (Negroponte) ∼ It's time that the CIA and FBI get over their rivalries abroad. (Lake)

Attitudinal differences surfaced as well. A former foreign service officer, commenting on his State Department colleagues, asserted:

…it very quickly becomes ingrained in them that they are to treat others with a sort of contempt. (Mora)

Several suggested a team approach to improve mission integration and effectiveness:

> What I intend to do is to take the persons and the resources that I have and try to build them into teams which are oriented to specific goals. (Kornblum) ~ A smart ambassador will play to the team's strength and devise a team very, very carefully. (Mora)

Listening

Some argued that the most important function of an embassy is listening:

> I don't mean listening simply to whether such-and-such a political party will gain in the next election in western Japan. I don't mean that kind of listening. I mean pulse listening. I mean sentiment listening. I mean wary listening, gripe listening, dream listening. (Hitchcock) ~ [The first priority of diplomacy is] to understand the society in its many dimensions. (Quainton) ~ One's information-gathering and analyzing staff would have to be increased and strengthened and given enough intellectual weight so that synthesis could be done. (Anable) ~ I would shift a great deal of my emphasis to deepening and widening the net. (Carter)

Reflecting the requirement for integrated analysis, several proposed

> ...dispensing with the false division between political work and economic work. (Newton) ~ It probably is not sensible to structure our reporting and analysis around concepts as general as politics and economics. (Quainton) ~ I haven't distinguished between the political and the economic, and I really would not inside the Embassy. (Schmitz) ~ I would probably not tinker much with the USIS post, though I would want to colocate it with the political and economic sections, which I would also want to meld in this mission. (Bray)

In contrast with commercial work, several suggested that economic reporting per se might be reduced:

> We've got this huge private sector that spends zillions of dollars doing that, and they do it better than the State Department is ever going to do it. Just buy everybody a Bloomberg. (Fukuyama) ~ I know this is kind of against the grain, but I'm not too sure how important an economic reporting function is. (Burt)

Commercial Diplomacy

Many demanded "a far more aggressive job in promoting American commerce, American sales overseas." (Gergen)

> I'd focus on trying to foster commerce rather than do-good programs. (Dyson) ~ I would very easily give the highest priority in our international diplomacy to the competitiveness of the United States. (LaPalombara)

Some argued that the function has been shortchanged and should be upgraded:

So, one thing I would think very seriously about in the commercial functions is trying to upgrade the kind of people who are in that function and strengthen the links between those people and the business community. (Burt)

There was, as well, a minority view on commercial diplomacy:

I would not be so inclined to promote narrow American commercial interests abroad in a particular place. (Ungar) ∼ I'm not sure what kind of role an embassy can play in the commercial field. (Mora)

Public Diplomacy

Many also made the case for strengthening the public diplomacy function:

I would want to strengthen the public communications area of the embassy so that the U.S. message is heard clearly. (Fouhy) ∼ We are astonishingly shortsighted in not strengthening the cultural and information and communication dimensions of our diplomatic services. (LaPalombara) ∼ I would clearly have a very strong public affairs presence. (Frost) ∼ What I would try to do is to strengthen the cultural program. (Fulbright)

On the other hand, there were a few voices of doubt:

To some degree I'd want to reduce the USIA kind of role. (Eagleburger) ∼ I guess I would downplay the public relations kind of spinning-message-type functions. (Dennis)

Intelligence

Several made persuasive cases for selectively reducing the intelligence function:

The problem with the intelligence gathering and analysis in embassies abroad is that it's not very good; the stuff I've seen is mediocre at best. (Burt) ∼ I would think the security side, the CIA side, all of that business could be grossly eliminated and phased down altogether. (Hauser) ∼ Most of the information we need is gained through an open source, by just contacting people on a day-to-day basis and then doing really good analysis. (O'Neill) ∼ I have considerable doubt about the importance to the United States of having military intelligence gathered through the attaché system. (Schmitz)

Information Systems

Some argued for establishing modern communication systems and for enhancing the use of technology:

I would certainly want to experiment with the use of encoded satellites. (Wick) ∼ My first priority would be to give them the tools they need to do their job more effectively, and that would mean very high speed access to the Internet, the ability to link with videoconferencing and e-mail. (Nelson) ∼ I would want to have some system set up whereby when things are happening, I would have intelligent and official backup who could let me know very rapidly and would use all the latest forms of information gathering to do this. (Anable)

Understanding and deploying the new interactive media as well as traditional media was also highlighted:

Understanding how to employ those capabilities, how to engage those capabilities, how to fight them if necessary is, I think, a new array of skills that are understood only in a limited and piecemeal fashion. (Schwartz)

Some commented on the danger of substituting technology for human contact and judgment:

Technology is an important tool, but it cannot substitute for person-to-person contact. (Chao) ∼ It's increased our ability to sit here and get a lot of information, a lot of data. But to understand, in a profound way, a way that's really useful, what's happening in that country, amazingly, thus far at least, it hasn't helped much. (Burnett)

Resources

A few respondents pointed to the growing disparity between State Department resources and those available to other federal agencies abroad:

The State Department is generally, these days, more deprived of sums than the others, which does create a kind of inequity within the embassy. (Kampelman) ∼ It is ironic, but probably the better-funded agencies are the ones that are not directly contributing to the country mission; they're the ones that are focusing on their own bureaucratic agendas. (Burt)

Several commented on the critical role that the right people can make in an embassy:

I would back the people who are the smartest, the most experienced, the most curious, the most interested, and know the most about the area in which they're representing this country. (Grossman) ∼ There are times when one person, with enough background and understanding of the country—its politics, its society, its religious and cultural factors—could be more important than the other 69 for determining what our national interests are and understanding the country. (Burnett)

Media and Information Technology

QUESTION: Larry Eagleburger has said that the Bush administration's decision to intervene in Somalia was greatly influenced by television coverage—and others have observed that our decision to withdraw was also precipitated by the media. Madeleine Albright told the Senate Foreign Relations Committee that "television's ability to bring graphic images of pain and outrage into our living rooms has heightened the pressure both for immediate engagement in areas of international crisis and immediate disengagement when events do not go according to plan." Diplomacy was traditionally conducted behind closed doors by a few people who spoke for their governments. Today diplomacy takes place in full public view with ever increasing public participation, largely facilitated by information technology—including telephones, faxes, the Internet, radio, and television. What are the major changes that information technology should bring to the conduct of diplomacy?

The CNN Effect

There was nearly unanimous agreement that the CNN effect, although not irrelevant, was less powerful than many commentators have assumed:

> My sense is that the so-called CNN effect is wearing off a bit here at home. (Gergen) ∼ I do not accept the inevitability of the consequences, nor do I accept even the analysis of the consequences of coverage. (Carter)

Although many agreed that the media can be a powerful force in decisionmaking—"Madeleine Albright's description is absolutely correct." (Eagleburger)—there was also broad agreement that the media's role is minimal when policy is clearly formed, articulated, and supported:

> The CNN effect refers to a situation where policy is not well defined, and a major visual image of a crisis situation catalyzes opinion and builds pressure for action where the administration either did not want to act or hasn't figured out what it wants to do. (Solomon) ∼ If that is going to cause American policy to change, then it seems to me that American policy is pretty damn weak in the first place. (Davidson)

Many, indeed, remarked on the positive effects of CNN:

> It's very useful that CNN is out there bringing realities home to the United States because it does engage the American public. (Lake) ∼ Once the population has access to pictures of suffering, there is clear support there for some intervention, some kind of intervention to change, to alleviate the suffering. (Powell) ∼ If scenes of carnage in Somalia and other places prompt American action, then I wonder why anyone would criticize it. (Mora) ∼ If you watched CNN during the Kuwait–Iraq War, there is no question that it was a good thing in the sense that it made it clearer to all of us what had transpired. (Eagleburger) ∼ CNN and the TV coverage, that's a fact of life. We're not going to change that, and that's wonderful. I, frankly, welcome it. (Lange)

Media Responsibility

In addition to their comments on the CNN effect, many criticized the evolving role of the media in international affairs coverage:

> What television tends to do is sensationalize the news and dumb down the news to the point where you are looking for the most intriguing, salacious, provocative stories. (Burt)

Others deplored the media tendency to cover complex issues with slogans or sound bites and to reduce coverage of international events:

> My own sense is that we could perform a considerable service to bring far more context to the coverage of this world. (Lawrence) ∿ I would like to see the media playing a much more positive and creative role in helping the American public understand the really central issues of American foreign policy. (Fromm) ∿ It would be very useful if television could do more to bring home to the American people what the realities are abroad. (Lake)

Behind Closed Doors

Several took issue with the question's assertion that diplomacy takes place today in full public view:

> You say that diplomacy is no longer conducted largely behind closed doors, is now out in the public forum. I'm not quite sure that's true. (de Borchgrave) ∿ The Oslo Accords, the Dayton Accords, many important decisions are made by the people responsible for them, conducting private negotiations. (Grossman) ∿ Most of the important business that I can think of that's been accomplished in the last 30 years has been accomplished behind closed doors in intense negotiations by parties who were being forced to come to the kinds of compromises which people say are impossible to do in the modern global world. (Carter)

Leadership

Even if negotiations are conducted in secret, information technology has broadened the concerned public and reduced the time between conclusion and public reaction. There was general agreement that policymakers must increasingly seek public support through information sharing and education—in a word, leadership:

> In many ways it places a much greater premium and demand for leadership. (Harrington) ∿ Just because the public is a player doesn't mean that leaders don't have a very important role to play as, indeed, leaders. (Grossman) ∿ It requires a president to be willing to challenge public opinion at any moment and to explain why he is challenging or she is challenging it. (Kampelman)

Immediacy

Several argued that the immediacy of the new media drives both public opinion and decisionmaking:

> Diplomats no longer have the luxury to ponder. (Roberts) ∿ The new phenomenon is the immediacy of the resulting public impact. (Bray) ∿ There's no way to get around the need for more rapid response, really almost immediate response to most events. (Duffey) ∿ What it does more than anything else is to speed up the decision cycle for those who are in a position to make a decision. (O'Neill)

Some suggested that recognition of this dynamic should provide diplomats sufficient time for thoughtful analysis and reaction:

> It needs to self-consciously be aware that this is the dynamic they're in and then look for those opportunities, the interstices, where they can still yet obtain some breathing room for the quieter exchange, especially some opportunity for reflection. (Hedblom) ∼ It puts a premium on policymakers, especially diplomats, to learn how to sort out information so they can keep their eye on what is critical and not be caught up on what is urgent. (Gergen)

Transparency

Several spoke of transparency as an aspect of the new media that is favorable to the United States:

> We are a society that has basically thrived on transparency. (Schwartz) ∼ The United States has always stood for the free flow of people, ideas, and information across international boundaries. And, lo and behold, that's now happening in ways far beyond the imaginings of any of us a short time ago. (Robison) ∼ It's going to be harder for people, nations, maybe even for terrorists, to organize themselves to mount an effect attack on our physical integrity to the degree that information is freely and universally available. (Bray) ∼ The creative opportunity is to use new global communication technology to build a sense of who we are, an image of our purposes and commitment, and make better investments in the long run. (Etheredge) ∼ We should use information technology to highlight our ideas, our notion of what is a civil society, what is democracy, how does one build a civil society, how does one build democracy. (Fouhy) ∼ This is a fantastic opportunity for mass education. It's a fantastic opportunity for a massive blunder, also. (Kalb)

Diplomacy of the Future

> One dimension of the diplomacy of the future is to recognize that Sergeant Friday was wrong. You never get the facts, and you never get all of the facts, and so we have to have a diplomatic service that acts as a counterbalance to what the media are delivering by way of images and other forms of communication to mass publics. (LaPalombara) ∼ [The profound effects of the media and information technology] heighten the need for carefully organized professional diplomacy. (Kornblum) ∼ We ought to be sure that these images which we receive are images which are reacted to by professionals who take into account those images but who also have a wider and broad base of knowledge on which to act and to inform our public. (McHenry) ∼ That requires more resources being given to the analytic function and distinguishing between information which is interesting or titillating and information which enables diplomats, governments, and others to understand. (Hemery)

Effects of Information Technology on Diplomacy

Respondents suggested several additional effects that information technology will have on diplomacy:

Whether one approves or disapproves of the fact that diplomacy is no longer in the hands of a small group of highly elite diplomats or not, that era is simply over. (Fouhy) ～ It is making diplomacy less elitist. (Bloch) ～ The other sense in which a very important change has occurred is far more subtle, and it has to do with the vastly broadened and more complex and fragmented international agenda. (Moose) ～ The Internet, faxes, international telephone calls have made it possible to create communities of a kind that didn't exist at the same level previously. I think we're in the process of a paradigm shift, a global paradigm shift, as people with common interests find ways to interact with each other and try to influence politics locally and internationally. (Cowan) ～ The key way that information technology is influencing diplomacy is by enabling people to talk back, giving them more power, and contributing to more democratization and free markets and having more influence on their governments. (Quainton) ～ E-mail is changing the environment of diplomacy. (Hocking) ～ I believe we will see development of desktop-to-desktop communications between governments. (Quainton) ～ The greatest impact available to us will be the new wireless infrastructure; the digital information age will change the way content is created and produced. (Wick) ～ The single most important impact in the long run will be that we are no longer the exclusive holder of information on certain topics. (Newton) ～ People will be tied together in ways that have never been envisioned before. (O'Neill) ～ Discussions will happen at lower levels within the bureaucracies. (Nelson) ～ Much more decisionmaking will take place in the center. (Newton) ～ The role of the media affords us the opportunity to exploit that transparency, to make possible the increasing use of that media to reveal that which we would wish to be revealed, or that which we'd wish to be seen. (Schwartz)

Requirements for Exploiting the New Technologies

A variety of suggestions were offered to exploit information technology in the service of diplomacy:

We now need a public affairs attention, a public information role to make sure the public is operating with all the facts that simply didn't exist before. (Johnstone) ～ You've got to have greater expertise in public diplomacy, the ability to get out there in front of these issues. (Anable) ～ You've got to be more skilled at using television, as explainers, as reassurers. (Anable) ～ Because television is so effective, it means that we have to pay much more attention to those things which are not televisable. (Schmitz) ～ State needs digital video teleconferencing facilities; they need the open, unclassified Internet. (Schneider) ～ We have not figured out a way to bring Internet to the desks of foreign service officers. We've got to solve that problem. (Moose) ～ Maintaining your home page is a major issue, a major dimension of public diplomacy. (Hocking) ～ The main thing it should be able to do for us is to make easier a lot of mechanical tasks of delivering information. (Burnett) ∿ One of the things it should or can do is to increase the possibility for the State Department to be proactive about moving information around to interested groups and parties. (Hedblom) ∿ We need to take into account the degree to which information technology broadly informs the American public on an almost instantaneous basis of foreign developments. (Pickering) ∿ Certain kinds of information gathering do not need to be done locally anymore. (Negroponte) ∿ So much of the trade reporting and so on can be done electronically. (Hitchcock) ∿ Right now, the best thing the State Department could do would be simply to get up to speed, get up to where everybody else is in terms of technology. (Burt) ∿ It is extremely important that people who represent the United States abroad be able to manage this new technology. (Kalb) ∿ We need to find ways to improve our own capacity to transmit internal information and to be able to do so in a way that provides us rapidly with a concise assessment of what's happening as well as suggestions as to how to respond. (Pickering)

A Rum-Soaked Old Honorary Consul

While considering the wonders of technology, we are reminded by both an information specialist and a former diplomat that there is no substitute for human judgment in diplomacy:

> I don't think the technology is going to replace human relations any time soon. (Dyson) ∿ If it had been the turn of the century and there had been some rum-soaked old honorary consul who had been sitting on the veranda of the hotel in the middle of Mogadishu, simply learning about what had been going on in the country for 20 years, he could have been a lot more help to Admiral Howe. (Burnett)

Communicating with Foreign Publics

QUESTION: I have one final question that reflects the increasing participation of foreign publics in decisionmaking. If diplomacy is no longer just state-to-state but people-to-people, what role has the federal government in facilitating diplomacy among interested publics here and abroad? In particular, when international issues involve the government, nongovernmental organizations, and the private sector, what should be done to ensure that we communicate effectively with foreign publics?

NGOs

Many respondents acknowledged the increasing influence of NGOs in international affairs and the need for government to communicate more effectively with them:

> They're becoming far more influential, they've become more important. (Burt) ∿ We have got to encourage nongovernmental organizations, the citizen outcry, the citizen's expressions of views. (Marks) ∿ We ought to be working with

NGOs that are international in character more than we do. (Gergen) ∽ The United States government should take the wise position of trying to partner with identifiable organizations at the national, the local, the regional, and certainly the transnational level. (Schneider) ∽ Good diplomats have increasingly welcomed into their work the responsible NGOs. (Hemery)

However, a few noted that State's communication with the NGOs is less than satisfactory:

NGOs in this country, the ones I am familiar with, don't specifically think of turning to the State Department, or to diplomats, to assist them in their work. (Klose) ∽ I happen to know the leadership of Amnesty and for them to have a meaningful conversation with the U.S. government is actually extremely difficult. (Schwartz)

International Exchanges

It is no surprise that many spoke of the value of international exchanges:

The Fulbright program and things like that have really paid off dozens of times over. (Nelson) ∽ It not only changed my life but has had some sort of impact on literally thousands of students who, in the last almost 45 years, have been through my classrooms. (LaPalombara) ∽ One of the things that makes me so terribly sad is that we have backed away from facilitating and encouraging that. (Robison) ∽ Governments have to encourage much more of that interaction—educational exchanges, cultural exchanges, facilitating travel. (Grossman)

Networking

A number of respondents spoke of the power of networking as a means of communication:

There is a major change in the sociology of influence. (Etheredge) ∽ Interaction is now much more complex, so it seems to me that we have an opportunity and a challenge and a need to change attitudes and habits of how we work with and through other institutions beyond governments if we want to get our purposes achieved in the world. (Quainton) ∽ I'd simply like to shift the USIA model, which has tended to be one-way outbound to the rest of the world and say, "Let's identify the purpose of the agency as relationship building." (Etheredge) ∽ If there's a role for the U.S. government, it is to be a source of information on some matters and to facilitate these kinds of contacts. (Fouhy) ∽ It's not necessary for the United States to play the role of a universal educator megaphone. (Fromm)

Technology

Again, respondents urged that information technology be exploited to strengthen international communication:

Embrace the new technology; don't be repelled by it. (Kalb) ∼ Information technology does allow us to get our message out to foreign publics much more effectively. (Nelson) ∼ What we have is an opportunity to leverage that strength along with our leadership in information technology and information content. (O'Neill) ∼ The new media are potentially very, very valuable because they do have enough richness to provide context. (Thorson) ∼ I'm increasingly convinced that the future progress of democracy and human rights, for example, will depend at least as much on the Internet and the communications revolution as it will on official American government policies in pushing other societies toward reform. (Lake) ∼ I am utterly supportive of the government funding Internet development and continuing its efforts in the conventional media as well. (Brown)

Agenda Setting

Several pointed to the government's responsibility to focus attention on salient issues by speaking with clarity:

> The real thing is clarity of purpose from the political leadership. (Kornblum) ∼ I believe it becomes more and more important that governments define their positions. (Moose) ∼ They ought to be speaking very clearly to that public on the ground in terms of why U.S. policy has done what it's done. (Davidson) ∼ What government can do best is to focus public attention on an issue. (Hitchcock)

Others spoke of the government's role in focusing its communications on selected publics:

> There is a power of convening—convening meetings, convening conferences—that's still much more persuasive or significant when exercised by the government than, say, [by] a private company. (Dennis) ∼ One of the most important roles of anyone in government is to figure out how to get the right people together. (Lawrence)

Communicating with U.S. Publics

Several respondents spoke with some passion about the need for better communication with U.S. publics:

> I will confess that my particular concern is that our people in the administration do not realize the danger to diplomacy by our continuing to keep close hold on what it is that we do and to convey the attitude that it's really no one's business who is not cleared to know what it is that we do. (Schmitz) ∼ A government that fails to treat its publics, domestic or foreign, as partners will be in trouble. (Bray) ∼ There is a real need for a much more aggressive public diplomacy inside the United States. (Quainton)

Reservations

Although the great majority agreed with the desirability of engaging foreign publics, a few suggested a quite modest role for the federal government:

I think it ought to be a fairly constrained role. (Eagleburger) ∼ I'm not sure that the federal government has much of a role in that. (Fouhy) ∼ The theme's changed so much now that I think the opportunity for hitting the wrong note and getting a backlash makes it a very, very dangerous kind of undertaking. I think it takes a different skill base than I find resident in most of the diplomatic corps. (Sheridan)

Another, who strongly supports a government role in communicating with foreign publics, also worried about capabilities:

The problem is the kind of mistake avoidance, error avoidance, that so much of the cultural tradition of American diplomacy is based on—that it is better to have a hundred errors of omission than one error of commission. (Harris)

Brave New Digital World

QUESTION: There may be a question you would like to answer that I haven't asked. What's bothering you? How are things different for you? What's frustrating you? What impact is technology having on you?

Communication Revolution

It is essentially democratic in its impulses and slightly demonic in its consequences. (Duffey) ∼ The dynamics of change at work today are far greater than any of us know. We are in a new epoch, based on contradictions, on uncertainties, and on what I call "fragmegration." (Rosenau)

Information Glut

Technology affords us too much information with too little understanding. (Fulbright) ∼ The number of inputs has expanded geometrically, and our ability to cope with those increased inputs has not really changed very much. (Eagleburger) ∼ The danger of this Information Revolution is that people spend all their time with short-term instant responses to everything, and nobody shuts the door and turns off the technology and thinks. (Anable) ∼ Even given the change in the pace of receiving information, I don't think our bodies have changed to absorb the damned stuff and to think it through. (Dennis)

Technology Gap

We are at a state where the technology is outrunning our ability to use it well. (Fouhy) ∼ The technology revolution is outpacing our ability to manage it. (Frost) ∼ People who really, really understand the substantive side, because they tend to be the older generation, are exactly the ones who are almost technology phobic. (Bloch) ∼ There is a tendency to remain passive in light of these super-duper, superhuman leaps that are occurring in the area of telecommunications, of accessing, classifying, retrieving, analyzing, communicating data. (LaPalombara)

State Department Lag

I'm concerned about the future of the foreign service. (Fitz-Pegado) ∼ We have a big challenge right now, caused by the communication revolution, to ensure that diplomacy continues to have a responsible image with its practitioners and with its public and not be allowed to be passed off as something which has largely outlived its usefulness and is now something merely quaint. (Schmitz) ∼ Established structures, established attitudes, established ways of doing business will not serve us well in the evolving and very complex world in which we have to operate. (Quainton) ∼ The present lack of effectiveness in many parts of our foreign affairs structure is, to some significant degree, the result of organizational dysfunction. (Moose) ∼ We have spent hundreds of millions for technology, and we don't have much to show for it. It's a real threat to the ability of the State Department to compete. (Harris) ∼ The main point is that we need now to have a really bottom-up look at our professional diplomacy. (Kornblum)

Personnel Conundrum

I think part of what we need is a return to the value and privilege of government service and government careers as being a noble undertaking. (Reid) ∼ Our top political leaders neglect filling our embassies in a timely way; they continue to appoint unqualified people to important diplomatic assignments. (Rielly) ∼ We have a rotten system for selecting ambassadors. (Burt) ∼ People are not rewarded for being good managers; they are rewarded for deals, for making their bosses look good. (Frost)

Other Global Perplexities

I'm frustrated right now in terms of American foreign policy, in part because I see a rise in isolationism, in part because I don't see leadership being exercised. (McHenry) ∼ One of the reasons the American public is so turned off by foreign policy is because nobody has articulated a vision in the last decades that makes any sense to them anymore. (Manilow) ∼ My greatest foreign policy concern is the lack of communication to the American people on the part of our government. (Kampelman) ∼ There's not a wide understanding of what I know to be the powerful place that U.S. international broadcasting has in helping set the table for diplomatic initiatives. (Klose) ∼ To what extent is the government enlisting our great corporations to achieve this wireless infrastructure, and to be able to be a catalyst for these various kinds of global broadcasting services and information conveyances? (Wick) ∼ Is it inevitable that the impact of this kind of technology on diplomacy is to actually reduce the sovereignty of the United States? (Schwartz)

Interviews

Anable, David; President, International Center for Journalists; September 12, 1997.

Bloch, Julia Chang; President, U.S.-Japan Foundation; September 17, 1997.

Bray, Charles W.; President, The Johnson Foundation; September 19, 1997.

Brown, Merrill; Managing Editor, MSNBC Online; September 23, 1997.

Burnett, Stanton H.; Senior Adviser, CSIS; August 6, 1997.

Burt, Richard; Chairman, IEP Advisors, Inc.; September 26, 1997.

Carter, Hodding; President, MainStreet; September 9, 1997.

Chao, Elaine; Distinguished Fellow, Heritage Foundation; July 28, 1997.

Cowan, Geoffrey; Dean, Annenberg School for Communication, University of Southern California; September 22, 1997.

Cutler, Lloyd N.; Senior Counsel, Wilmer, Cutler & Pickering; September 25, 1997.

Davidson, Ralph P.; President, Davidson and Associates; September 3, 1997.

de Borchgrave, Arnaud; Senior Adviser in Residence, CSIS; July 31, 1997.

Dennis, Patricia Diaz; Senior Vice President, SBC Communications, Inc.; September 29, 1997.

Duffey, Joseph; Director, United States Information Agency; September 11, 1997.

Dyson, Esther; Chairman, EDventure Holdings, Inc.; September 29, 1997.

Eagleburger, Lawrence S.; Senior Foreign Policy Advisor, Baker, Donelson, Bearman, & Caldwell; August 28, 1997.

Etheredge, Lloyd S.; Director, International Scientific Networks Projects, Policy Sciences Center, Inc.; July 17, 1997.

Fitz-Pegado, Laurie J.; Vice President, Global Gateway Management, Iridium; August 14, 1997.

Fouhy, Edward M.; Executive Director, Pew Center for Civic Journalism; August 13, 1997.

Fromm, Joseph; Chairman, U.S. Committee, International Institute for Strategic Studies; September 9, 1997.

Frost, Ellen L.; Senior Fellow, Institute for International Economics; July 11, 1997.

Fukuyama, Francis; Hirst Professor of Public Policy, George Mason University; September 15, 1997.

Fulbright, Harriet Mayor; Executive Director, President's Committee on the Arts & Humanities; October 1, 1997.

Gergen, David R.; Editor at Large, *U.S. News & World Report;* August 6, 1997.

Grossman, Lawrence K.; Author, *The Electronic Republic: Reshaping Democracy in the Information Age;* September 15, 1997.

Harrington, Anthony S.; Senior Partner, Hogan & Hartson; September 18, 1997.

Harris, F. A. "Tex"; Past President, American Foreign Service Association; August 27, 1997.

Hauser, Rita E.; President, Hauser Foundation; September 22, 1997.

Hedblom, Milda K.; Director, Telecommunications and Information Forum, Humphrey Institute, University of Minnesota; August 29, 1997.

Hemery, John; Director, Centre for Political and Diplomatic Studies, Oxford, United Kingdom; July 22, 1997.

Henrikson, Alan K.; Director, Fletcher Roundtable, Fletcher School of Law and Diplomacy, Tufts University; July 25, 1997.

Hitchcock, David I.; Senior Associate, CSIS; October 2, 1997.

Hocking, Brian; Director, Centre for International and European Studies, Coventry University, United Kingdom; July 22, 1997.

Johnstone, Craig; Director of Resources, Plans and Policy, Department of State; August 18, 1997.

Kalb, Marvin; Edward R. Murrow Professor of Press and Public Policy, Harvard University; September 24, 1997.

Kampelman, Max M.; Chairman, American Academy of Diplomacy; August 25, 1997.

Klose, Kevin; Director, International Broadcasting Bureau, United States Information Agency; July 30, 1997.

Kornblum, John; Assistant Secretary of State for European Affairs, Department of State; July 16, 1997.

Lake, Anthony; Distinguished Professor, Georgetown University; August 5, 1997.

Lange, John D.; Managing Director, Lange, Mullen, and Bohn, LLC; August 27, 1997.

LaPalombara, Joseph; Wolfers Professor of Political Science and Management, Yale University; October 8, 1997.

Lawrence, David; Publisher, *Miami Herald;* September 16, 1997.

Manilow, Lewis; Chairman, U. S. Advisory Commission on Public Diplomacy; August 11, 1997.

Marks, Leonard H.; Of Counsel, Cohn and Marks; August 1, 1997.

McHenry, Donald F.; Distinguished Professor, Georgetown University; September 10, 1997.

Moose, Richard M.; Senior Fellow, The CNA Corporation; October 1, 1997.

Mora, Alberto; Of Counsel, Greenberg Traurig; August 12, 1997.

Negroponte, John; Special Coordinator for Post-1999 Presence in Panama, Department of State; August 6, 1997.

Nelson, Mike R.; Director, Technology Policy, Federal Communications Commission; August 1, 1997.

Newton, Alastair; Deputy Head, Policy Planning Staff, Foreign & Commonwealth Office, London; July 24, 1997.

O'Neill, Richard P.; Deputy Director, Strategy and Policy, Office of the Assistant Secretary of Defense, C³I, August 26, 1997.

Pickering, Thomas; Under Secretary for Political Affairs, Department of State; August 14, 1997.

Powell, Adam Clayton III; Vice President for Technology and Programs, Freedom Forum; August 1, 1997.

Quainton, Anthony C. E.; Director General of the Foreign Service, Department of State; August 7, 1997.

Reid, Ogden; President, Council of American Ambassadors; September 9, 1997.

Rielly, John E.; President, The Chicago Council on Foreign Relations; September 24, 1997.

Roberts, Walter R.; Commissioner, U. S. Advisory Commission on Public Diplomacy; September 8, 1997.

Robison, Olin; President, Salzburg Seminar; September 30, 1997.

Rosenau, James N.; University Professor of International Affairs, George Washington University; August 4, 1997.

Schmitz, Charles A.; Chairman, Global Business Access, Ltd.; July 29, 1997.

Schneider, Michael; Executive Director, Steering Committee on the Future of the Fulbright Education Exchange Program; July 31, 1997.

Schwartz, Peter; President, Global Business Network; October 3, 1997.

Sheridan, Edward; President, Sheridan Management Group; September 18, 1997.

Solomon, Richard H.; President, United States Institute of Peace; August 8 and 11, 1997.

Thorson, Stuart J.; Director, Global Affairs Institute, Maxwell School, Syracuse University; August 22, 1997.

Ungar, Sanford J.; Dean, School of Communication, American University; August 19, 1997.

Wick, Charles Z.; President, Charles Z. Wick & Associates; September 19, 1997.

Zorthian, Barry; President, Public Diplomacy Foundation; July 18, 1997.

State Department Congressional Testimony

O N SEPTEMBER 17, 1998, Under Secretary of State for Management Bonnie R. Cohen testified before the Senate Task Force on Function 150. In her testimony, she addressed the scope and complexity of State Department interests. Excerpts follow:

Let me start this on a personal note. Before taking this job as Under Secretary for Management at the State Department, I had had seven or eight professional jobs, including four years as Assistant Secretary at the Department of the Interior. All of which is to say, I thought of myself as a fairly seasoned professional. Yet—and I know this is a cliché, but some clichés are nevertheless profoundly true—nothing prepares you to be called at 4:00 in the morning to be told that two US embassies in Africa have been bombed within 10 minutes of each other. And as you drive through the empty streets at that time of the morning, you are praying that by the time you get to the office the number bombed won't be three, four, or five. And then when it is still only two and you are slightly relieved, the actual horror starts to seep in, even as you are putting the other embassies on alert and coordinating rescues or medical supplies.

Secretary Albright said when she took office that diplomacy can't be conducted on the cheap, and that has been brought home to us with a vengeance. The $2.1 billion State Department operating budget is now significantly less than 1 percent of the federal budget, and if you take into account inflation, it is less than it was in real dollar terms in 1986. And yet some would argue that our children's future depends to a larger extent on the success of the State Department than many other Federal activities.

In my first year at the State Department, I have been struck again and again by the scope and complexity of our operational requirements and the paucity of our resources. To carry out its global responsibilities the Department of State maintains about 260 diplomatic and consular posts which provide the necessary infrastructure for 27 other US Government agencies with more than 300 different activities in about 160 countries. These embassies and consulates provide an essential link between the United States and the governments and peoples of other countries. With a few exceptions, the United States follows the principle of universality by having a diplomatic mission in every country with which we have diplomatic relations. Even with modern communications, there is no effective substitute for having a physical presence throughout the world. Our diplomatic posts not only carry out our diplomatic relations with foreign leaders, they also assist American citizens, support US business and develop the extensive local contacts that are essential to effective diplomacy.

The Department employs a workforce of about 23,000 employees, 14,000 Americans and 9,000 foreign nationals; it manages financial operations in more than 140 different foreign currencies; and it communicates with world leaders in over 60 foreign languages. Approximately 60 percent of our employees work overseas. In FY 1997, the Department processed over eight million visa applications and issued six million passports. In 1997, the Department sent and received nine million pounds of classified and unclassified mail.

The break-up of the Soviet Union resulted in a drop in military spending, but we did not make the concomitant expansion in our diplomatic budget that was required to maintain the peace. Instead, cost cutting or flat budgets have had serious consequences for our ability to carry out our mission well. For example:

—In 1998, the Department had more than 300 vacancies world-wide, especially in critical areas like information management and consular operations. These vacancies result in an overworked and insufficiently trained staff.

—Between FY-88 and today, Diplomatic Security positions have declined by about 12 percent, from approximately 1,390 to about 1,230 worldwide. From 1988 to 1996, the total number of Special Agent positions also dropped by 12 percent. In 1990, about 275 Diplomatic Security Special Agents were serving as Regional Security Officers in overseas posts, compared to about 250 today.

—Since 1986, the Department has opened over 40 new posts in response to changing foreign policy priorities. The demise of the Soviet Union alone has led to the creation of 18 new embassies and five other posts. These were established with limited new funding, by reallocating existing money, and with no additional positions, including overseas security positions. As one result, the Bureau of Diplomatic Security was compelled to reduce security staffing at some embassies in order to meet the staffing and security requirements of the new posts in what were assumed to be higher risk areas.

—In 1997, the Department processed about three million cables, and the volume of e-mail continues to climb exponentially. However, our telecommunications to the majority of posts is slow at best. While we have begun to turn the corner with Congress's stern prodding and financial support, we still have a long way to go. Overseas, approximately 50 percent of our telephone systems, 60 percent of our radio equipment, 65 percent of our classified computers and 35 percent of our unclassified computers would be obsolete by 2000 without your help.

—Americans would be surprised, if not appalled, at the state of disrepair of many of our buildings overseas. For example, our posts in China are overcrowded, technologically starved and seriously in need of improvements in safety and security. At our Embassy in Beijing, sewer gas leaks through the building. And yet, in the past year alone, American staffing from all US government agencies increased by 15 percent in China, and is likely to increase even more.

—The Department has received virtually no appropriations for capital projects since FY-95. Proceeds from worldwide property sales, which averaged $46 million in the FY-94 to 97 period, from a low of $13.9 million in FY-96 to about $112 million in FY-97, were supposed to finance facilities construction. (The approximately $112 million total includes $30 million from sales in Korea which are now in dispute.)

However, even if such funds were devoted exclusively to new embassies in Germany and China, for instance, they would not finance our requirements for Berlin and Beijing, let alone address the rest of our real building problems including vulnerable locations. Especially given the most recent events, it appears likely that the Department will require the support of Congress in the near future to establish a fully funded, long-term capital program.

As to security, as you know, we have been consulting with Congress over the past few weeks on an emergency security supplemental. It does not make sense to turn our embassies into fortresses—even if we could, which is doubtful—or into places where we put security so far ahead of promoting American ideals that we cannot do our business properly. The Administration will be seeking an emergency supplemental appropriation for the State Department and other agencies to help reestablish our diplomatic facilities in Nairobi and Dar es Salaam and better protect the thousands who work in—and visit—our facilities around the world.

Before I go into more detail on that, however, let me give you a broader indication of problems we face. Security, while vitally important and central to everything we do, is only part of our overall infrastructure deficit. Over the years, prioritizing our various infrastructure needs and meeting emergency requirements has meant that many important areas have been short-changed. For example:

Information Technology. The construction of an information infrastructure to support American diplomacy in the 21st century is one of my most critical and urgent objectives as Under Secretary of State for Management. In today's fast-moving, increasingly interdependent and networked world, American diplomats must have modern, secure information technology to respond to world events. Providing this technology to the State Department means deploying the modern information networks needed for rapid, secure Department communications worldwide; strengthening our information systems security, and ensuring Year 2000 compliance for our critical communication and computer systems.

The significant decrease in resources allocated to the State Department since the end of the Cold War has left us vulnerable and less prepared to carry out diplomacy in the information age. Flat and declining budgets for State from 1993 through 1997 resulted in an overall erosion of the Department's infrastructure, creating critical staffing and training gaps and unmet information technology needs. At the same time, during this period of stagnant resources, the demand for new information technology and skills grew exponentially. As a result, we have been unable to make the investment needed to equip and staff our communications and computer centers worldwide adequately with modern information technology.

Personnel. We are desperately short of people. Everywhere I have traveled in this job, I have met truly dedicated, talented personnel who are overworked and in some cases, lacking the necessary training to do their jobs effectively and efficiently. This critical problem was exacerbated by downsizing, expansion of diplomatic posts, and burgeoning work, especially in the consular areas.

The breakup of the Soviet Union and Yugoslavia led to the creation of 23 new posts, for which the Department received no additional positions and only limited funding. One hundred fifty five American positions were shifted to staff these new posts, and their staffing has now grown to 286 State personnel. We have also increased our presence in the Far East with expansion in China and the establishment of US relations with Cambodia and Vietnam. With the opening of these posts, we now need more language qualified officers, creating an additional burden on our system. Officers who will serve at hard language posts generally need to be assigned to one to two years of training in order to reach an acceptable proficiency level. During this training period, they are not available for other assignments, thus placing more strain on staffing requirements.

To further exacerbate our staffing situation, we project that there will be a significant increase in Civil Service retirements. By the year 2010, over 1,200 out of 5,000 Civil Service employees at State will be eligible to retire. These departures will dramatically undermine the Civil Service continuity in the senior level management and policy positions.

At the same time our worldwide presence was expanding, the State Department downsized. From 1992–97, the Department reduced American employment by 11 percent, from about 12,000 to about 10,800. This has had a significant impact on our ability to carry out our mission. Unlike some cabinet level agencies, the Department has no large grant programs—60 percent of our operating budget goes to salaries and related personnel costs. People are our chief asset.

Training. Our goal is to maintain a highly skilled, diverse workforce which can take the Department into the next century. A focus on long-term career development and training in specific skills is critical for achieving this goal. However, in a recent survey, almost 40 percent of the approximately 1,500 language designated positions were filled with officers who did not have requisite language skills. Staffing gaps at posts have increased pressure for the Director General to grant language waivers, and in FY-97, the Department granted over 80 waivers. During FY-98, the Department granted about 125 waivers to those who did not meet the language requirements of their assigned positions. In addition, we provided almost no administrative, political, economic, consular or computer training for the approximately 9,000 foreign national employees who play a critical role in supporting our missions overseas.

Reorganization. As part of the reorganization effort we developed last year with Congress, we continue to work closely with USIA and ACDA to plan for their full integration with the Department. We look forward to getting the legislative authority we need to implement this. The reinvention plan of April 1997, devised by the Vice President and approved by the President, strikes a sound balance. It will enhance policy effectiveness and better utilize the special missions and skills of USIA and ACDA and their very talented people. We are also cooperating with USAID on some steps in the administrative area.

Integration for USIA is a big task, involving several thousand American and foreign staff, but it also is beginning to move ahead. In a pilot project, USIA's Europe Office is co-locating with our European Bureau. We're considering merging security offices, and USIA junior officers are now receiving orientation training alongside State junior officers. We want to co-locate more public diplomacy units with policy-makers on key issues, and plans are being developed to merge management systems.

Much preparatory work on integration was done last year by an interagency task force, enabling some progress to be made. But we need legislation to bring the maximum benefits of integration.

Security. I want to focus now on security issues—a critically important area, and one that has been very much on everyone's mind since the ghastly bombings in East Africa last month. We are submitting a supplemental budget request to address security problems, and I will go into some details of that request in a few moments.

What have we done since the bombings? First, I know that all of you are particularly interested in knowing what steps we have taken since the bombings in East Africa in order to address problems there and potential problems elsewhere. Let me detail, to the extent that I can in a public forum, what we have done and are doing. Since the terrorists who are interested in replicating the carnage of East Africa elsewhere in the world are also listening to what I have to say, I know you will understand my inability to mention certain specifics.

—We have deployed interagency Embassy Security Assessment Teams (ESATs) to evaluate the physical security of our potentially vulnerable embassies and consulates.

—Additional Diplomatic Security (DS) agents, security engineers, and Seabees have been sent to Nairobi and Dar es Salaam to support those posts as they recover and rebuild. Additional agents have also been dispatched to other posts around the world where we believe they are needed.

—The Bureau of Diplomatic Security has established an emergency coordination group as a focal point for all security action issues, and Regional Security Officers (RSOs) around the globe are reporting daily on their posts' security situation as well as on needed security enhancements.

—Posts have responded to a Department cable with requests for short, medium, and long-term security improvements, all of which are being evaluated. We are working with host governments to immediately implement short term quick fixes.

We have come to recognize that we must modify our perimeter defense strategy with regard to overseas posts. We are establishing and will implement a security strategy that, within the limits of fiscal realities and physical constraints, will be employed globally to harden the perimeters of our diplomatic and consular establishments.

Conclusion. Following the East Africa bombings, and after she escorted home the remains of our fallen American colleagues, Secretary Albright said that "…America will continue to be present around the world, wherever we have interests to defend, friends to support, and work to do." She also promised that "America will not be intimidated" and "…that we will do all we can to protect our diplomatic and military people around the world." The supplemental budget request for security will go a long way toward fulfilling that promise, and I hope that I may count on you and the Task Force to support this request and future investments in diplomacy.

For, in a larger sense, diplomacy is America's first line of defense. While military prowess is necessary to secure our national security, the conduct of US diplomatic and consular relations with the rest of the world is what makes our nation a force for peace and stability in a still highly unstable and dangerous world. Modest—but prudent—investments in diplomacy and sustainable development are leveraged many times over as we work to prevent conflict, open markets, promote democracy, enhance communications, and protect the environment. These efforts, funded by the Function 150 account, go a long way to decrease the possibilities of more costly conflicts later, as well as to ensure the prosperity and well-being of the American people.

Advisory Panel

Cochairs

RICHARD BURT is chairman of IEP Advisors and has had a career in diplomacy, government service, and international business. He served in the State Department as assistant secretary of state and director of the Bureau of Political-Military Affairs. He also was the chief nuclear arms negotiator and U.S. ambassador to the Federal Republic of Germany.

OLIN ROBISON is president of the Salzburg Seminar and is president emeritus of Middlebury College. He chaired the U.S. Advisory Commission on Public Diplomacy from 1977 to 1981. He was a Peace Corps administrator and a member of the office of the deputy under secretary of state for political-military affairs during the Lyndon B. Johnson administration.

Project Director

BARRY FULTON is a senior associate at CSIS. He served as associate director for information and as acting associate director for educational and cultural affairs of the United States Information Agency. He has been an adjunct professor at American University and has written and spoken on public diplomacy and change management.

Advisory Panel Members

DAVID ANABLE is the president of the International Center for Journalists, a Washington-based nonprofit organization that conducts worldwide training, exchange, and fellowship programs for journalists. He was previously the chairman of the Boston University School of Journalism and, before that, was foreign editor and then managing editor of the *Christian Science Monitor*.

JULIA CHANG BLOCH is a visiting professor of the Institute of International Relations and executive vice chairman of the American Studies Center at Peking University, Beijing, China. She has had a career in diplomacy, government service, banking, and philanthropy. She served as ambassador to the Kingdom of Nepal, USAID assistant administrator, group executive vice president at Bank of America, and president of the U.S.-Japan Foundation.

CHARLES W. BRAY is the former president of the Johnson Foundation, deputy director of USIA, ambassador to Senegal, and chairman of the American Foreign Service Association. He received the President's Distinguished Service Award in 1984 and the Freedom Foundation Award in 1980.

MERRILL BROWN is editor in chief of MSNBC on the Internet. His career includes stints as a business writer and Wall Street correspondent for the *Washington Post* and editor in chief of the award-winning monthly magazine, *Channels*. He was a founder and senior vice president of Courtroom Television Network.

STANTON H. BURNETT is a senior adviser at CSIS and its former director of studies. He was counselor and director of research of USIA as well as public affairs counselor in Rome and at NATO. An scholar of Italian issues, he is the coauthor of *The Italian Guillotine: "Operation Clean Hands" and the Overthrow of Italy's First Republic.*

HODDING CARTER is president of the John S. and James L. Knight Foundation. Formerly president of MainStreet, a television production company, he was the Knight Professor of Journalism at the University of Maryland. A former newspaper editor, television anchor and commentator, and syndicated columnist, he was the State Department spokesperson during the Jimmy Carter administration.

ELAINE CHAO is a distinguished fellow at the Heritage Foundation. She was formerly president of United Way of America, director of the Peace Corps, deputy secretary of the Department of Transportation, and chairman of the Federal Maritime Commission. She was also a banker with Bank of America and Citicorp.

GEOFFREY COWAN is dean of the Annenberg School for Communication at the University of Southern California and professor of journalism and law. He was director of the Voice of America from 1994 to 1996 and is the author of *The People v. Clarence Darrow.*

LLOYD N. CUTLER is senior counsel of Wilmer, Cutler & Pickering. He was counsel to the president in 1994 and from 1979 to 1980. He was ambassador for maritime boundary negotiations with Canada and special counsel to the president on ratification of the SALT II treaty. He holds numerous awards including honorary degrees from Yale and Princeton.

RALPH P. DAVIDSON is president of Davidson & Associates. He serves as chairman of the Romanian-American Foundation and is a trustee and director of the American University in Bulgaria. He is the retired chairman of Time, Inc. and a past chairman of the John F. Kennedy Center.

ARNAUD DE BORCHGRAVE is director of the CSIS global organized crime project and editor at large of the *Washington Times*. He is the former editor in chief of the *Washington Times* and former senior editor and chief foreign correspondent of *Newsweek*. He is coauthor of *The Spike* and *Monimbo* and the recipient of 10 major international journalism awards.

PATRICIA DIAZ DENNIS is senior vice president and assistant general counsel for regulation and public policy for SBC Communications Inc. She served as a commissioner of the Federal Communications Commission from 1986 to 1989, a member of the National Labor Relations Board from 1983 to 1986, and assistant secretary of state for human rights and humanitarian affairs from 1992 to 1993.

WILSON DIZARD JR. is a senior associate at CSIS and author of six books on international communications, including *Old Media, New Media* and *Meganet*. A former adjunct professor at Georgetown University and foreign service officer, he has authored some 60 articles, reports, and surveys on communications.

DIANA LADY DOUGAN is senior adviser and chair of International Communications Studies at CSIS. She served in the State Department with the rank of ambassador as the first statutory coordinator for international communications and information policy. She is a former marketing director for Time, Inc. and an award-winning television producer.

ESTHER DYSON is chairman of EDventure Holdings and investor in several high-tech startups in Central Europe and Russia, including APP Group and Netbeans (Prague); Poland Online and Computer Land Poland (Warsaw); Middle Europe Networks and E-Pub (Budapest); and Dator, DPI, IBS, and Terralink (Russia). She is the author of *Release 2.0: A Design for Living in the Digital Age*.

LAWRENCE S. EAGLEBURGER is senior foreign policy advisor at Baker, Donelson, Bearman, and Caldwell. He served as secretary of state and deputy secretary of state in the Bush administration. Prior assignments include ambassador to Yugoslavia, under secretary of state for management, and acting assistant secretary of defense for international security affairs.

LLOYD S. ETHEREDGE is a trustee and project director at the Policy Science Center, a public foundation in New Haven, Connecticut. Earlier he taught at MIT for eight years and was director of graduate studies for international relations at Yale. Recent publications include *Can Governments Learn?* and *Politics in Wired Nations*.

LAURI J. FITZ-PEGADO is vice president for global gateway management at Iridium, LLC. Before joining Iridium she was assistant secretary and director general of the U.S. and Foreign Commercial Service, where she transformed the organization by stressing client-driven service and corporate-style management. She also served as a foreign service officer with USIA.

EDWARD M. FOUHY is executive director of the Pew Center on the States, an Internet-based research and information service. A reporter, producer, and news executive for more than 25 years, he previously served as CBS News vice president and news director and as ABC News vice president. He was executive producer of both the 1988 and 1992 presidential debates.

Joseph Fromm is chairman of the U.S. committee of the International Institute for Strategic Studies; fellow, Johns Hopkins Foreign Policy Institute; member of the strategic advisory panel of the CIA; and member of the technical advisory committee of the Center for Naval Analysis. He is a former assistant editor, foreign correspondent, and contributing editor of *U.S. News & World Report*.

Ellen L. Frost is a senior fellow at the Institute for International Economics. She has served as counselor to the U.S. Trade Representative and as deputy assistant secretary of defense. She is the author of *Transatlantic Trade: A Strategic Agenda* and *For Richer, For Poorer: The New U.S.-Japan Relationship*.

Francis Fukuyama is Hirst Professor of Public Policy at George Mason University. A former RAND Corporation analyst and State Department official, he is the author of *Trust: The Social Virtues and the Creation of Prosperity* and of *The End of History and the Last Man*.

Harriet Mayor Fulbright is the executive director of the President's Committee on the Arts and Humanities. She previously served as the assistant director of the Congressional Arts Caucus, the executive director of the Fulbright Association, and the president of the Center for Arts in the Basic Curriculum.

William B. Garrison Jr. is director of International Communications Studies at CSIS. He is the author of case studies on telecommunications restructuring in several nations and is a lecturer on telecommunications policy.

David R. Gergen is editor at large at *U.S. News & World Report*, a regular conversationalist on PBS's NewsHour with Jim Lehrer, and a visiting professor at Duke University. He served in the Clinton White House as counselor to the president and as special adviser to the president and the secretary of state. He spent eight years in the White House as an adviser to former presidents Nixon, Ford, and Reagan.

Lawrence K. Grossman is president of PBS Horizons Cable. He is the former president of NBC News and former president and chief executive officer of PBS. He is the author of *The Electronic Republic: Reshaping Democracy in the Information Age* and is a regular columnist for the *Columbia Journalism Review*.

Anthony S. Harrington is a senior partner of Hogan & Hartson and has been a founder and director of several telecommunications companies. He is chairman of the President's Intelligence Oversight Board and vice chairman of the President's Foreign Intelligence Advisory Board. He was a member of the Commission on the Roles and Capabilities of the U.S. Intelligence Community.

Rita E. Hauser is president of the Hauser Foundation and an international lawyer. She chairs the International Peace Academy and the advisory board of the RAND Center for Middle East Public Policy. She is a director of many organizations involved in international conflict resolution, diplomacy, and strategic studies.

MILDA K. HEDBLOM is a professor, lawyer, and consultant. She is a senior associate and director of the Telecommunications and Information Society Forum at the Hubert H. Humphrey Institute of Public Affairs, University of Minnesota, and is a professor of politics and media at Augsburg College, Minneapolis. She was previously the Marks Fellow in International Communications at CSIS.

ALAN K. HENRIKSON is director of the Fletcher Roundtable on a New World Order at the Fletcher School of Law and Diplomacy, Tufts University, where he teaches American diplomatic history. He is an affiliate of Harvard University's Weatherhead Center and was Lloyd I. Miller visiting professor of diplomatic history at the Department of State. He is the author of *Diplomacy for the 21st Century: 'Re-Crafting the Old Guild'*.

DAVID I. HITCHCOCK is a senior associate at CSIS and commissioner of the U.S.-Japan Friendship Commission. A 35-year veteran of the foreign service, he holds the Edward R. Murrow Award for Excellence in Public Diplomacy. He is a contributor to the *Los Angles Times, Christian Science Monitor*, and *Washington Quarterly*.

MARVIN KALB is director of the Joan Shorenstein Center on the Press, Politics and Public Policy and the Edward R. Murrow Professor of Press and Public Policy at the John F. Kennedy School of Government, Harvard University. Over a distinguished 30-year career, he has been chief diplomatic correspondent for CBS News and NBC News and was moderator of *Meet the Press*.

MAX M. KAMPELMAN is president of the American Academy of Diplomacy, chairman of the Georgetown University Institute for the Study of Diplomacy, and vice chairman of the United States Institute of Peace. He was ambassador and head of delegation to the negotiations on nuclear and space arms and the CSCE.

KEVIN KLOSE is currently president and chief executive officer of National Public Radio. At the time of this study he was director of international broadcasting for the United States Information Agency. He is a former president of Radio Free Europe/Radio Liberty, director of Radio Liberty, and Moscow bureau chief of the *Washington Post*. His books include the award-winning *Russia and the Russians: Inside the Closed Society*. He is a Eurasia Foundation board member.

ANTHONY LAKE is distinguished professor in the practice of diplomacy at the Edmund A. Walsh School of Foreign Service at Georgetown University. He was assistant to the president for national security affairs from 1993 to 1997. He has taught at Amherst and Mount Holyoke, served as a foreign service officer in the Department of State, and authored several books including *Somoza Falling: A Case Study of Washington at Work* and *Our Own Worst Enemy: The Unmaking of American Foreign Policy*.

JOHN D. LANGE is managing director of Lange, Mullen & Bohn, LLC, which provides strategic and tactical advice and counsel for international project management, investment, and foreign exchange strategies. He served as director of foreign exchange operations at the U.S. Treasury Department and as chief negotiator for the United States on official trade finance.

JOSEPH LAPALOMBARA is the Arnold Wolfers Professor of Political Science and Management at Yale University. He has chaired Yale's department of political science and directed its Institution for Social and Policy Studies. He is a member of the American Academy of Arts and Sciences, a past vice president of the American Political Science Association, and a widely recognized author and consultant.

LEWIS MANILOW is chairman of the United States Advisory Commission on Public Diplomacy. He serves on the board of the National Democratic Institute for International Affairs and is chairman of its Middle East committee. He is the honorary president of the Goodman Theater in Chicago.

LEONARD H. MARKS is chairman of Radio Free Europe/Radio Liberty Fund, Inc.; chairman of the Fund for the Endowment of the Diplomatic Reception Rooms, Department of State; and treasurer and director of the World Press Freedom Committee. He is a former director of the USIA, incorporator of the Communications Satellite Corporation (COMSAT), and chairman of the International Conference on Communications Satellites (INTELSAT).

DONALD F. MCHENRY is distinguished professor in the practice of diplomacy at Georgetown University, president of the IRC Group, and director of several corporations. He served as ambassador and U.S. permanent representative to the United Nations and has been affiliated with the Brookings Institution, the Council on Foreign Relations, and the Carnegie Endowment for International Peace.

RICHARD M. MOOSE is a senior fellow at the CNA Corporation. He served as under secretary for management at the State Department, senior vice president of American Express, managing director of Shearson Lehman Brothers, and assistant secretary of state for African affairs. He also held senior positions with the National Security Council and Senate Committee on Foreign Relations.

ALBERTO MORA is of counsel to Greenberg Traurig, where he practices in the field of international law. A member of the U.S. Broadcasting Board of Governors, he formerly served as general counsel of USIA and as a foreign service officer in the Department of State.

RICHARD P. O'NEILL is director of the Highlands Forum, a cross-disciplinary group of national leaders from government, industry, academia, media, and the arts who examine the impact of the Information Age on economics, organizations, international relations, and security. He was formerly the deputy for information operations strategy and policy, office of the assistant secretary of defense (C^3I).

ERIK R. PETERSON is senior vice president and director of studies at CSIS, where he also holds the William A. Schreyer Chair in Global Analysis. Before joining CSIS, he was director of research at Kissinger Associates.

ADAM CLAYTON POWELL III is vice president for technology and programs of the Freedom Forum. He has served as vice president of news at National Public Radio, manager of network radio and television news for CBS News, and executive producer for Quincy Jones Entertainment. He is the coauthor of *Lethargy '96: How the Media Covered a Listless Campaign.*

ANTHONY C. E. QUAINTON is executive director of the Una Chapman Cox Foundation. During a 38-year foreign service career he served as director general of the foreign service and ambassador to Peru, Kuwait, Nicaragua, and the Central African Republic.

OGDEN REID is president of the Council of American Ambassadors. He served as a member of Congress from 1961 to 1974. He was ambassador to Israel, president and editor of the *New York Herald Tribune,* and vice chairman of GTS Duratek. He is a board member of General Physics and of Royce Labs.

JOHN E. RIELLY is president of the Chicago Council on Foreign Relations. He has served as a foreign policy assistant to Vice President Hubert Humphrey and as a consultant to the Ford Foundation. He is the editor of *American Public Opinion and U.S. Foreign Policy,* which has been published every four years since 1975.

WALTER R. ROBERTS is senior advisor to the U. S. Advisory Commission on Public Diplomacy. He is a former commissioner of the Public Diplomacy Advisory Commission and former associate director of USIA. He is the author of *Tito, Mihailovic and the Allies, 1941–45.*

JAMES N. ROSENAU is university professor of international affairs at George Washington University. A former president of the International Studies Association, he is the author of *Turbulence in World Politics: A Theory of Change and Continuity* and *Along the Domestic–Foreign Frontier: Exploring Governance in a Turbulent World,* as well as numerous other books and articles.

CHARLES A. SCHMITZ is chairman of Global Business Access, Ltd., an international consulting firm, and president of Global Access Institute. He served in the Department of State's office of the legal advisor, as a U.S. foreign service officer overseas, and as vice president of AFSA.

MICHAEL SCHNEIDER is director of the Syracuse Maxwell Washington International Relations Semester. Previously he held senior policy positions in USIA and the Department of State. He was also executive director of the Commission on Future Fulbright Exchange.

PETER SCHWARTZ is the president of Global Business Network and contributing writer of *Wired* magazine. He was a planner for Royal Dutch/Shell and futurist with SRI International. He is the author of *The Art of the Long View: Planning for the Future in an Uncertain World* and coauthor of "The Long Boom."

JAMES SCHWOCH, the 1997–1998 Leonard Marks Fellow in International Communications Policy at CSIS, is on the faculty of Northwestern University, where he holds appointments in the Center for International and Comparative Studies and in the department of communication studies. He has written extensively about U.S. foreign policy and international communications.

EDWARD SHERIDAN is president of the Sheridan Management Group. He chairs the committee on government liaison of the Financial Executives Institute. He headed corporate finance at a predecessor to Paine Webber, was director of acquisitions at Westinghouse, and chief financial officer at Fairchild.

RICHARD H. SOLOMON is president of the United States Institute of Peace. He served previously as assistant secretary of state for East Asian and Pacific affairs and as U.S. ambassador to the Philippines. He headed the social science department at the RAND Corporation for 10 years and is the author of 6 books, including *Nuclear Dilemmas and Asian Security*.

STUART J. THORSON is director of the Global Affairs Institute and professor of international relations and political science at the Maxwell School of Citizenship and Public Affairs at Syracuse University. He also holds a courtesy appointment in computer and information science at Syracuse University. His current research is focused on uses of information technology in support of democratic governance.

SANFORD J. UNGAR is dean of the school of communication at American University. A journalist in Washington for nearly three decades, he has been a staff writer for the *Washington Post*, managing editor of the magazine *Foreign Policy,* and host of *All Things Considered* on National Public Radio. He is the author of *Africa: The People and Politics of an Emerging Continent* and *Fresh Blood: The New American Immigrants,* among other books, and editor of *Estrangement: America and the World.*

CHARLES Z. WICK is president of Charles Z. Wick & Associates, consultant to Rupert Murdoch, and board member of Town Hall, Los Angeles World Affairs Council, and the Margaret Thatcher Foundation. He was the director of USIA during the Reagan administration and was director of News Corporation and News America Holdings.

WALTER B. WRISTON is former chairman and chief executive officer of Citicorp/Citibank. He is the author of *Twilight of Sovereignty* and *Risk and Other Four Letter Words.*

BARRY ZORTHIAN is president of the Public Diplomacy Foundation and a partner at Alcalde & Fay. He is a former vice president of Time Inc. and minister-counselor at the U.S. mission to Saigon from 1964 to 1968. He also served in India as a foreign service officer and at the Voice of America as a program manager.

The CSIS International Communications Studies (ICS) Program focuses on the policies, politics, and technologies of all forms of information that move across borders electronically. Each year the program targets a series of specific and timely issues in the field of international communications that warrant strategic attention from the private as well as public sector. The goal of the program is to foster more informed and effective decisionmaking and strategic planning in both government and industry. The ICS program also actively develops initiatives and recommendations that promote the role of electronic communications in support of democratic values and free market economies.

Senior Adviser: Diana Lady Dougan
Program Director: William B. Garrison Jr.
Project Director: Barry Fulton

We would like to extend a special thanks to our ICS corporate sponsors and contributors that help make these publications possible.

Corporate Sponsors:	Ameritech	Media One
	AT&T	Mitsubishi
	Bell Atlantic	NYNEX
	Cable & Wireless	PanAmSat
	GE Information Services	Sprint/Global One
	Hughes	Teleglobe
	LCI International	

Corporate Contributors:	Ascend Communications	IBM
	BT	Matsushita
	Deutsche Telecom	MCI WorldCom
	EDS	SBC Communications
	GE Fund	Xerox
	Global One	

Underwriting/funding for the Diplomacy in the Information Age study: The Annenberg Foundation

For additional information on the project, including summaries of meetings, conference presentations, and transcripts of interviews, see <http://www.csis.org/ics/dia>.

International Communications Studies Program
Center for Strategic and International Studies
1800 K Street, NW, Washington, DC 20006
Telephone: (202) 775-3263
Fax: (202) 775-0898
E-mail: ics@csis.org
Web site: http://www.csis.org/ics/